Australian Curriculum

A student workbook

Leanne Bondin & Adam Kealley

First published in 2023

Insight Publications Pty Ltd
3/350 Charman Road
Cheltenham Victoria 3192
Australia

Tel: +61 3 8571 4950
Fax: +61 3 8571 0257
Email: books@insightpublications.com.au

www.insightpublications.com.au

A catalogue record for this
book is available from the
National Library of Australia

Australian Curriculum English Year 10 / Leanne Bondin and Adam Kealley

ISBN:

9781922771711

Edited by Lisa Neale
Cover by Melisa Paredes
Internal design by Melisa Paredes
Typesetting by Sardine
Proofread by Penny Mansley
Printed by Markono Print Media Pte Ltd

Contents

Note to teachers

The *Australian Curriculum English* series is designed to assist student development of English skills, knowledge and understanding in interesting, engaging ways. The series aligns with Version 9.0 of the Australian Curriculum, ensuring that the Literature, Language and Literacy strands of the curriculum, as well as their sub-strands and threads, are seamlessly integrated and well balanced across the units of work. Each text in the series covers the entire curriculum content for its corresponding year level at least once, and in most instances several times, in order to highlight the varied approaches available to teachers and their students. Relevant Australian Curriculum content is specified in the introduction to each unit.

Each *Australian Curriculum English* book comprises 12 units, each of which is centred on a unifying theme, text type or significant English skill. Cumulatively, the units provide ample opportunity for students to practise their writing, reading, listening, speaking and viewing skills. The units can be completed in any order; teachers may find it useful to dip in and out of units in ways that complement their established teaching and learning programs.

The units include a number of text extracts, from familiar 'classics' to more contemporary and original texts. The extracts have been selected for their potential to illustrate particular curriculum content in action; teachers are encouraged to examine the texts independently to assess their suitability for their specific school context or cohort. While each unit includes multiple activities related to the unit focus, the final two units in the book closely target the specific comprehension strategies and grammar, punctuation and word knowledge specified in the Australian Curriculum English 7–10.

A range of colour-coded '**Check for understanding**' and '**Reflecting and discussing**' activities are embedded within the content of units 1–10. These activities are designed to:

- help students strengthen and deepen their understanding of the concepts covered
- encourage students to reflect carefully upon the content in relation to their own lives and experiences
- facilitate meaningful whole-class or small-group interactions and discussion around the content.

Several '**Get creative**' activities within units 1–10 prompt students to create their own texts in a range of forms by practising writing, speaking and creating for different audiences and purposes. All activities make ideal classroom and/or homework tasks. Many of the written activities included can be completed within the fill-in lines provided.

As English teachers ourselves, we appreciate the importance of practical and helpful resources that supplement our own classroom practices and assist students to master essential curriculum content and skills. We sincerely hope that this series does just that for you and your students.

To access suggested solutions to the activities in this workbook, please email us at sales@insightpublications.com.au

UNIT 1

Personal essays

You are probably familiar with *analytical essays* – the type that you write in English in response to a studied film, novel or short story. There are lots of other types of essays too, including *personal essays*. A personal essay is a form of non-fiction reflective writing that allows the author to express their thoughts, experiences and feelings on a particular topic or event. This unit will help you to examine the features of personal essays and to understand how they can reveal the writer's values.

In this unit, you will learn:

- to analyse and evaluate language features in personal essays
- how authors organise ideas within their personal essays to achieve a purpose
- approaches to writing your own personal essay.

Curriculum content

Australian Curriculum content description	Content code
Understand that language used to evaluate, implicitly or explicitly reveals an individual's values.	AC9E10LA02
Analyse and evaluate how language features are used to implicitly or explicitly represent values, beliefs and attitudes.	AC9E10LY03
Analyse and evaluate how authors organise ideas in texts to achieve a purpose.	AC9E10LY04

Personal essay features

Personal essays are different from other types of essays because they focus on the writer's unique experiences and reflections, rather than arguing a specific point or analysing another text. This type of essay is highly subjective and is usually written in the first person, using the **pronoun** 'I' to share the writer's perspective. A list of common personal essay features is below.

pronoun A word that takes the place of a noun (e.g. I, me, he, she, herself, you, it, that, they, few, many, who, whoever, someone, everybody, and many others)

- personal anecdotes
- first-person pronouns (I, me, myself)
- vivid descriptions of experiences or memories
- sensory details
- recollections of dialogues
- paragraphs of varied lengths
- informal language and conversational tone
- a final reflection on the topic

1.1 Reflecting and discussing

Discuss the following questions in pairs, in small groups or with the whole class as directed by your teacher.

1 Have you ever read or written a personal essay?

2 What do you think is meant by describing personal essays as 'highly subjective'?

3 Review the features of personal essays listed above. What other types of texts include these features?

Personal essays share features with other types of writing, like memoirs and autobiographies, that reflect on individual experiences and observations. However, there are some key differences between these forms. Personal essays often resonate with readers on both an emotional and an intellectual level by connecting their reflections to wider cultural and social issues or events. Memoirs and autobiographies are primarily **narratives**, whereas personal essays are not, though they may still include personal anecdotes or reflections on personal experiences. While personal essays can vary considerably in length, most range between a few paragraphs and a few pages.

narrative The selection and sequencing of events or experiences, real or imagined, to tell a story to entertain, engage, inform and extend imagination, typically using an orientation, complication and resolution

Examples of personal essays

Essayists – the authors of essays – often compile their essays into collections. The following titles are examples of either individual essays or essay collections.

Everywhere I Look (2016) by Helen Garner

'On Experience' (2008) by David Malouf

'Notes on an Exodus' (2016) by Richard Flanagan

'A Room of One's Own' (1929) by Virginia Woolf

'Two Ways of Seeing a River' (1883) by Mark Twain

Me Talk Pretty One Day (2000) by David Sedaris

Slouching Towards Bethlehem (1968) by Joan Didion

1.2 Check for understanding

Select any two of the essays or collections mentioned above. Conduct some online research about each one and record some of the main topics, issues or events that each one explores.

Title of essay/collection: ______________________________

____

____

____

Title of essay/collection: ______________________________

____

____

____

Voice in personal essays

Many of the essay writers previously listed are well known for their distinctive authorial voices. The **voice** of the author is the personality that speaks through their writing, and it may be apparent across their whole body of work. Voice can be very distinctive in its **style** or **tone**.

voice The distinct personality of a piece of writing; the individual writing style of the composer, created through the way they use and mix various language features (e.g. a narrative using a child's voice)
style The distinctive language features, text structures and/or subject matter in a text which may shape meaning, be enjoyed for its aesthetic qualities or distinguish the work of an author, period etc.
tone The mood created by the language features used by an author and the way the text makes the reader feel

1.3 Reflecting and discussing

Discuss the following questions in pairs, in small groups or with the whole class as directed by your teacher.

1 How might you describe the voice of an author who includes lots of comical jokes in their writing?

2 How might you describe the voice of an author who mocks or pokes fun at society in their writing?

3 How might you describe the voice of an author who reflects on the beauty of the Australian landscape in their writing?

The author's voice in a personal essay is, of course, personal. But just like someone's speaking voice, an author's personal voice in their writing can have distinctive elements.

1.4 Check for understanding

Locate and record definitions of the following terms, which can often be used to describe the authorial voice created in personal essays.

introspective: ______________________________

reflective: ______________________________

insightful: ______________________________

observational: ______________________________

strident: ______________________________

critical: ______________________________

The purpose of personal essays

Personal essays aim to connect with the reader, offering reflections on the writer's observations or experiences. They often provide interesting, thought-provoking **perspectives** on specific subjects and issues. Like most writing, personal essays also aim to entertain readers by creating an engaging tone, interesting descriptions and effective control of language.

perspective A lens through which the author perceives the world and creates a text, or the lens through which the reader or viewer perceives the world and understands a text

Case study: 'Laugh, Kookaburra'

David Sedaris is a popular American humorist and writer. His essay 'Laugh, Kookaburra' was first published in *The New Yorker* magazine in 2009. Although written by an American, it was reprinted in *The Best Australian Essays* in 2009, as it deals with a tourist's experience of Australia. Read the opening paragraphs of 'Laugh, Kookaburra' and answer the following questions.

I've been to Australia twice so far, but according to my father I've never actually seen it. He made this observation at the home of my cousin Joan, whom he and I visited just before Christmas last year, and it came on the heels of an equally aggressive comment. 'Well,' he said, 'David's a better reader than he is a writer.' This from someone who hasn't opened a book since Dave Stockton's *Putt to Win*, in 1996. He's never been to Australia, either. Never even come close.

'No matter,' he told me. 'In order to see the country, you've got to see the countryside, and you've only been to Sydney.'

'And Melbourne. And Brisbane,' I said. 'And I have too gone into the country.'

'Like hell you have ...'

I hate to admit it, but my dad was right about the countryside. Hugh and I didn't see much of it, but we wouldn't have seen anything were it not for a woman named Pat, who was born in Melbourne and has lived there for most of her life. We'd met her a few years earlier, in Paris, where she'd come to spend a mid-July vacation. Over drinks in our living room, her face dewed with sweat, she taught us the term, 'shout', as in 'I'm shouting lunch'. This means that you're treating, and that you don't want any lip about it. 'You can also say, "It's my shout", or "I'll shout the next round",' she told us.

We kept in touch after her visit, and when my work was done, and I was given a day and a half to spend as I liked, Pat offered herself as a guide. On that first afternoon, she showed us around Melbourne, and shouted coffee. The following morning, she picked us up at our hotel, and drove us into what she called 'the bush'. I expected a wasteland of dust and human bones, but it was nothing like that. When Australians say 'the bush', they mean the woods. The forest.

1.5 Check for understanding

1 Sedaris establishes a strong authorial voice in the essay. Suggest three **adjectives** that could be used to describe the tone of this voice.

____

adjective A word class that describes, identifies or quantifies a noun or a pronoun, e.g. two (number or quantity), my (possessive), ancient (descriptive), shorter (comparative), wooden (classifying)

2 List three **contractions** that appear in the extract. How does using contractions help to create Sedaris' tone of voice?

___

___

3 Although Sedaris does not directly comment on his feelings towards his father, what impression does their dialogue convey about their relationship?

___

___

4 What is the main experience being commented on in the extract?

___

___

5 What is the main idea being communicated about this experience?

___

___

___

6 What do you think is the overall purpose of the personal essay by Sedaris, based on the extract provided?

___

___

contraction An abbreviated version of a word or words, often formed by shortening a word or merging 2 words into one (e.g. doctor: Dr; do not: don't)

Values, beliefs and attitudes

A personal essay frequently reveals something about the writer's identity, such as the social groups they belong to, as well as their values, attitudes and beliefs or those in society at large. Each of these terms is defined below.

Values
Values are principles, ideals or standards that individuals or groups consider important in their lives. Common values include honesty, respect and equality.

Attitudes
Attitudes are a person's feelings or outlook towards people, issues or situations. They are often shaped by values and beliefs.

Beliefs
Beliefs are ideas or convictions that individuals or groups consider true or real. They are often based on personal experiences, knowledge, cultural teachings or religious doctrines.

Australian writer Helen Garner's personal essay collection *Everywhere I Look* explores her identity as an elderly person and other people's the reaction to her and others in this social group. The Western value of youth and the contemporary, dismissive attitude towards elderly people are apparent in some of Garner's essays. Various beliefs are also highlighted, such as the conviction that elderly people can make a valuable contribution to society.

'Laugh, Kookaburra' by David Sedaris also tells us something about his personal identity, including his values, attitudes and beliefs.

1.6 Reflecting and discussing

Discuss the following questions in pairs, in small groups or with the whole class as directed by your teacher.

1 How much has Sedaris chosen to reveal about himself in the extract that you have read from 'Laugh, Kookaburra'?

2 What kind of person has Sedaris presented himself as?

3 What values, attitudes and beliefs does Sedaris express in the extract?

The essay 'Laugh, Kookaburra' looks with interest at some of the differences in English language usage between Australia and America. Sedaris shows a writer's delight in learning new Australian words. He explains 'the bush' to his mostly American readers as 'the woods' or 'the forest'.

1.7 Check for understanding

Fill in the table below, giving equivalent American and Australian terms for these words:

American	Australian	American	Australian
cotton candy			autumn
	nappy	janitor	
	chemist shop	dumpster	
pacifier		flip flops	
sidewalk			holiday
elevator			biscuit

Similes, metaphors and analogies

Later in his essay, Sedaris reflects on his encounter with a kookaburra, writing the following description.

> The thing was as big as a seagull, but squatter, squarer, and all done up in earth tones, the complete spectrum, from beige to dark walnut. When seen full on, the feathers atop his head looked like brush-cut hair, and that gave him a brutish, almost conservative look. If owls were the professors of the avian kingdom, then kookaburras, I thought, might well be the gym teachers.

In this paragraph, Sedaris gives his readers an idea of the bird's size and colour in a lively, vivid way. He uses analogy, sometimes in the form of similes, to help create **imagery** and encourage readers to visualise the appearance of the kookaburra.

Revise your understanding of these **language features** by reading their definitions and an example of each in the following table.

imagery Visually descriptive or figurative language to represent things including objects, actions and ideas in ways that appeal to the senses of the reader or viewer
language features Features that support meaning e.g. clause- and word-level grammar, vocabulary, figurative language, punctuation, images. Choices vary for the purpose, subject matter, audience and mode or medium

Language feature	Definition	Example
simile	a comparison between two things that uses 'as' or 'like'	'The thing was as big as a seagull.'
metaphor	a figure of speech that compares two dissimilar objects by presenting one thing as another	'You are my sunshine.'
analogy	a comparison between two things that doesn't necessarily use simile or metaphor	'If owls were the professors of the avian kingdom, then kookaburras, I thought, might well be the gym teachers.'

1.8

Check for understanding

1 Some similes are considered clichés because they are so overused that they become **idioms** (recognisable, common expressions). Draw lines to complete the following similes that have become idioms due to their overuse.

as pretty as	a daisy
as sharp as	a pancake
as free as	a tack
as flat as	a bird
as fresh as	a picture

2 These similes can sometimes lack interest for readers because of their overuse. Create some more original similes using the same starters.

a as pretty as ______

b as sharp as ______

c as free as ______

d as flat as ______

e as fresh as ______

3 Identify whether the following examples are similes or metaphors.

a Her laughter bubbled up like a sparkling stream. ______

b It was electrifying to watch the concert. ______

c He's broken up about losing his job. ______

d The exam room was a pressure cooker of nerves and anticipation.

______

e The sun hung in the air like a blazing orange lantern. ______

idiom An expression whose meaning does not relate to the literal meaning of its words (e.g. 'They went out to paint the town red')

Organisation of ideas

The ways in which writers structure their personal essays can vary considerably. One of the main **purposes** of personal essays is to reflect meaningfully on an experience or observation, so they often begin with an introduction to the topic being explored before teasing out ideas about the topic in the body of the essay. Introspective moments of reflection and analysis, in which the writer reflects on the significance of their experiences, are woven throughout. Personal essays usually finish with a concluding paragraph or comment on the broader significance of the topic.

purpose An intended or assumed reason for a type of text

The following figure summarises the ways in which the ideas in a personal essay can be organised.

Introduction	• Begin with an engaging opening that grabs the reader's attention. • Introduce the central theme or topic of the essay. • Use an anecdote, a vivid description or a rhetorical question to hook the reader.
Body paragraphs	• Delve into your experiences, thoughts and emotions related to the topic. • Focus on a specifc aspect or point in each paragraph, providing supporting details, examples or anecdotes. • Include dialogue, sensory details and/or introspective reflections. • Think about how you can vary paragraph length; sometimes, very short paragraphs can add impact.
Conclusion	• Leave the reader with a lasting impression by providing a sense of closure through reflecting on the wider significance of the topic. • Consider ending with a final thought, a call to action or a throught-provoking question.

Using transitions to connect ideas

Transitional **phrases** and **connectives** allow a writer to move smoothly from one idea to the next. These features can enhance the flow and **cohesion** of a personal essay. Some transitional phrases and connectives are listed in the following table under the functions they perform in an essay.

phrase A group of words often beginning with a preposition but without a subject and verb combination (e.g. 'on the river'; 'with brown eyes')
connective Words linking, and logically relating ideas to one another, in paragraphs and sentences indicating relationships of time, cause and effect, comparison, addition, condition and concession or clarification
cohesion Grammatical or lexical relationships that bind different parts of a text together and give it unity. It is achieved through devices such as reference, substitution, repetition and text connectives

Adding ideas	Contrasting ideas	Showing cause and effect	Sequencing ideas	Summarising ideas
Furthermore	However	Consequently	Firstly	Ultimately
Moreover	By contrast	As a result	Secondly	To summarise
Additionally	Alternatively	Therefore	Lastly	All in all
Also	On the other hand	Thus	Subsequently	In the end
In addition	Conversely	Accordingly	Finally	In summary

1.9 Get creative

Plan and draft your own personal essay, following the steps below.

1 Select a topic for your personal essay by brainstorming a list of possible topics and then selecting your favourite. A few topics have been suggested to get you started.

a Reflect on a travel experience or journey and its impact on your values.

b Examine the significance of nature or the natural landscape in your life.

c Explore the concept of success in our society and its influence on you.

2 Answering the following questions will help you reflect meaningfully on your topic. Ensure that your answers are woven into the final part of your essay.

a What has this experience or topic taught you about yourself?

b How has this experience or topic clarified or challenged your values, beliefs and attitudes?

c What are the broader significance and impact of this experience or topic in society at large?

3 Following the organisational approaches listed earlier, draft your personal essay in your English notebook.

4 Use the checklist below to improve the quality of your personal essay.

Personal essay self-edit checklist	Tick when complete
Have you followed the organisational guide in the diagram to structure your personal essay clearly?	
Does your essay contain an engaging, distinctive sense of voice, in which your personality shines through? Think of some adjectives to describe this voice.	
Does each of your paragraphs and points connect to the next one, using transitional phrases/connectives to make the writing cohesive and guide the reader through your thoughts?	
Have you used interesting similes, metaphors or analogies to create vivid imagery and descriptions?	
Have you re-read and edited your essay for clarity, coherence, punctuation, spelling and grammar?	
Have you asked for feedback from teachers, peers or family members to improve your writing?	

UNIT 2

Poetic personas

We can learn a lot about others and their circumstances through literature. This unit will explore the ways in which poetry and other texts can be used to create representations of people, groups and places. You will observe how poetic language can work to include or exclude certain social groups and examine the aesthetic qualities of poems. Although the main focus in this unit is on representations of identity in poetry, other text types will also be referenced to help you understand the concept of national identity.

In this unit, you will learn:

- how poems can have empowering or disempowering effects on people
- to analyse representations of identity in poems
- how voice and other literary devices influence responses to poetry.

Curriculum content

Australian Curriculum content description	Content code
Understand how language can have inclusive and exclusive social effects, and can empower or disempower people.	AC9E10LA01
Analyse representations of individuals, groups and places and evaluate how they reflect their context in literary texts by First Nations Australian, and wide-ranging Australian and world authors.	AC9E10LE01
Compare and evaluate how 'voice' as a literary device is used in different types of texts, such as poetry, novels and film, to evoke emotional responses.	AC9E10LE06
Analyse and evaluate the aesthetic qualities of texts.	AC9E10LE07

National identity

'National identity' refers to the sense of belonging and cultural pride shared by individuals within a country. It includes the concepts of shared culture, history, language, traditions and **values** that bind people together as members of a particular nation.

The collective memories of a nation also contribute to its identity, because they help shape an understanding of a country's past, present and future. National identity encourages unity, social cohesion and a collective identity with others.

2.1 Reflecting and discussing

Discuss the following questions in pairs, in small groups or with the whole class as directed by your teacher.

1 What historical events, achievements and policies have shaped Australian national identity?

2 What national symbols and icons contribute to Australian national identity?

3 What shared values and beliefs make up Australia's national identity?

4 What **stereotypes** are usually projected by Australians in film and literature?

values Ideas and beliefs specific to individuals and groups
stereotype An oversimplified idea about a person or group and believing that all people in that group are the same, e.g. a stereotype of women might assert that they are all gentle and caring, while a stereotype of men might assert that they can't share their feelings

Representations of Australian identity

'Representation' is the way in which people, events, issues or subjects are depicted in a text. Texts such as films, songs, advertisements, novels, memoirs, paintings, short stories and poems are not necessarily accurate portrayals of the real world; rather, they are constructions or versions of reality.

Many texts give representations of Australian national identity by creating familiar depictions that are recognisable within our collective sense of self. These representations comprise the types of people Australians are, including their values, interests and beliefs.

2.2

Check for understanding

1 Draw lines in the table below to connect each of the familiar features of Australian identity on the left with its common representations on the right.

Features of Australian identity	Common representations
ANZAC spirit	the bush, beaches and the outback; activities like camping, surfing, bushwalking and barbecues
First Nations cultures	the idea of a 'fair go' for everyone; endorsement of fairness and equal opportunities, regardless of people's background or economic position
sporting culture	a laid-back and irreverent attitude; a sense of humour and cheekiness
egalitarian values	activities such as swimming and surfing; cricket, AFL and rugby matches
outdoors lifestyle	the rich cultural heritage of First Nations people, such as art, music, storytelling and spiritual connections to the land; impactful events and policies, such as the Stolen Generations
multiculturalism	Australian and New Zealand Army Corps soldiers during World War I; personal qualities like courage, resilience and mateship
larrikinism	people from various ethnic backgrounds engaging in their traditions, cuisines and celebrations

2 Some representations of national identity become so common and recognisable that they can be thought of as tropes, stereotypes, character archetypes or adopted personas. Find definitions for these words.

a trope:

____

____

b stereotype:

____

____

c archetype:

____

____

d persona:

____

____

3 The following films have created some familiar representations of Australian identity. Use your prior knowledge of them or watch the trailers online and identify which of the representations they may contain from the previous list.

a *The Castle* (1997) directed by Rob Sitch ______

b *Rabbit-Proof Fence* (2002) directed by Phillip Noyce (adapted from the memoir *Follow the Rabbit-Proof Fence* by Doris Pilkington Garimara) ______

c *Gallipoli* (1981) directed by Peter Weir ______

d *Looking for Alibrandi* (2000) directed by Kate Woods (adapted from the novel by Melinda Marchetta) ______

e *The Club* (1980) directed by Bruce Beresford (adapted from the play by David Williamson) ______

4 Other types of texts contain the common representations of Australian identity listed above. Identify which of them may be present in the following texts.

a 'The Man from Snowy River' (1890), poem by Banjo Paterson

______

b 'The Drover's Wife' (1892), short story by Henry Lawson

______

c The Ned Kelly Series (1946–1947), paintings by Sidney Nolan

______

d *The Pioneer* (1904), painting by Frederick McCubbin

______

Inclusive and exclusive language

Language can have both inclusive and exclusive social effects. This means that certain words or phrases can make some social groups feel included by providing them with a sense of acceptance, belonging and shared identity; however, certain words or phrases can also exclude some social groups and leave them feeling alienated or marginalised. Language can therefore empower or disempower people.

Poets frequently adopt personas through which to speak and communicate with **audiences**, meaning the persona and the poet are not the same person. A poet's thoughts may be reflected through their constructed persona, but sometimes a poet may adopt a persona completely at odds with their own personality and **perspective**.

audience An intended or assumed group of readers, listeners or viewers that a writer, designer, filmmaker or speaker is addressing

perspective A lens through which the author perceives the world and creates a text, or the lens through which the reader or viewer perceives the world and understands a text

With this idea in mind, read the poem below titled 'Be Good, Little Migrants', written by Uyen Loewald. Loewald was born in Vietnam in 1940, later moving to the United States and then migrating to Australia in 1970.

Be Good, Little Migrants

Be good, little migrants
We've saved you from starvation
war, landlessness, oppression
Just display your gratitude
but don't be heard, don't be seen

Be good, little migrants
Give us your faithful service
sweep factories, clean mansions
prepare cheap exotic food
pay taxes, feed the mainstream

Be good, little migrants
Use leisure with prudence
sew costumes, paint murals
write music, and dance to our tune
Our culture must not be dull

Be good, little migrants
We've given you opportunity
for family reunion
equality, and status, though
your colour could be wrong

Be good, little migrants
Learn English to distinguish
ESL from RSL
avoid unions, and teach children
respect for institutions

Be good, little migrants
You may fight one another, but
attend Sunday School, learn manners
keep violence within your culture
save industry from criminals

Be good, little migrants
Intelligence means obedience
just follow ASIO, CIA
spy on your fellow countrymen
hunt commies for Americans

Be good, little migrants
Museums are built for your low arts
for your multiculturalism
in time, you'll reach excellence
Just waste a few generations.

2.3 Check for understanding

1 What do you think is the main idea of the poem? Tick the correct answer.

a to encourage migrants to be more grateful for the opportunities they have been given ☐

b to express frustration and anger at the plight of new immigrants ☐

c to instruct migrants how to behave in their new countries ☐

2 The persona, or speaker, claims to have 'saved' the migrants and 'given' them benefits. Does the poem lead you to agree that the persona is noble and generous? Explain your response.

3 The poem paints a picture of migrants who have a very low, marginalised position in the society that claims to welcome them. Identify the ways in which the poem represents migrants as occupying an inferior social position.

4 In stanza 3, what attitude does the persona show towards the culture and art that migrants bring from their original countries?

5 Re-read the instructions that the speaker gives to the migrants about conforming to mainstream culture in stanzas 5 and 6. Are these reasonable suggestions? Provide reasons for your answer.

6 Loewald's use of the word 'we' is an example of inclusive language. Who do you think the persona is identifying with when they say 'we': the dominant social group or a minority group? How can you tell?

7 How do you think such a simple word as 'we' has the capacity to empower some social groups and disempower others?

Another way in which language can both include and exclude people is through words and phrases used by a specific group. For example, the **jargon** used in certain professions, such as law and medicine, enables those within those professions to communicate about the finer points of their work but can intimidate and exclude those who don't understand it. Similarly, the use of slang can be a way for young people to separate themselves from their parents.

jargon Technical words specific to a certain group, such as medical or legal jargon

2.4 Reflecting and discussing

Discuss the following questions in pairs, in small groups or with the whole class as directed by your teacher.

1 Brainstorm other ways in which language can be used to bond members of a group and/or exclude outsiders.

2 Can you think of examples from your own experience in which language has these effects?

Voice and persona in poetry

Voice is a distinct quality created in different types of texts, such as poetry, novels and film. It can be used to evoke strong emotional responses, such as compassion, anger or contempt. In poetry, the voice of the persona can be described according to its **tone** and the personality that it projects.

voice The distinct personality of a piece of writing; the individual writing style of the composer, created through the way they use and mix various language features (e.g. a narrative using a child's voice)
tone The mood created by the language features used by an author and the way the text makes the reader feel

2.5 Check for understanding

1 The persona in the poem 'Be Good, Little Migrants' repeatedly describes the migrants as 'little' and repeats the imperative instruction 'Be good.' Circle the **adjectives** below that best describe the tone that these **language features** create for the persona. Use a dictionary to help you if necessary.

condescending	admiring	patronising
respectful	arrogant	accepting

2 Provide reasons for your selections above by explaining what connotations, or associated meanings, are generated by the word 'little' and the instructions given in the poem.

3 Why has Loewald made the persona plural, using the word 'we'?

4 How can you tell that the voice is that of a persona and not the voice of the poet herself?

5 Loewald expresses the ideas in the poem using irony; that is, she states opinions that are contrary to her own. Why do you think she uses irony rather than expressing her real views about the treatment of migrants?

6 Explain your emotional reaction to the voice of the persona in this poem. Provide reasons for your answer.

adjective A word class that describes, identifies or quantifies a noun or a pronoun, e.g. two (number or quantity), my (possessive), ancient (descriptive), shorter (comparative), wooden (classifying)
language features Features that support meaning e.g. clause- and word-level grammar, vocabulary, figurative language, punctuation, images. Choices vary for the purpose, subject matter, audience and mode or medium

The poem 'Be Good, Little Migrants' suggests that conforming to the written or unwritten rules of society can be seen as a virtue, allowing groups and activities to operate smoothly. People often conform out of a desire to fit in and be accepted, or because they wish to avoid the consequences of *not* conforming.

Some people argue that being constrained by social expectations can sometimes lead people to suppress their unique identities and sense of self. In her poem 'Warning', Jenny Joseph writes about the joy of throwing off conformity as she ages.

> When I am an old woman I shall wear purple
>
> …
>
> I shall go out in my slippers in the rain
> And pick flowers in other people's gardens
> And learn to spit
>
> …
>
> You can wear terrible shirts and grow more fat
> And eat three pounds of sausages at a go

The persona ultimately realises, though, that conformity is necessary for the functioning of society.

> But now we must have clothes that keep us dry
> And pay our rent and not swear in the street
> And set a good example for the children.

2.6 Get creative

In your English notebook, craft your own poem that explores the concept of conformity and the expectations of a particular social group, such as teenagers or a sporting team.

Analysing aesthetic qualities

Like other types of literature, poetry can be analysed for its **aesthetic** qualities – the features that contribute to its artistic appeal. Three key aesthetic qualities associated with poems are listed below.

aesthetic Concerned with a sense of beauty or an appreciation of artistic expression

rhythm	• Devices such as rhyme, metre and repetition can create the cadence and rhythmical musicality of poetry. • Sound devices like onomatopeia, **alliteration** and **assonance** can maintain or disrupt the rhythm of poetry.
imagery	• Vivid sensory imagery can be created to engage the reader's senses and imagination. • Imagery can include visual, auditory, olfactory, tactile and gustatory images.
figurative language	• Figures of speech such as personification, **metaphors**, **similes** and **metonymy** can convey complex ideas and evoke emotions. • Figurative language conveys meanings and interpretations from the literal meaning in poetry.

alliteration A recurrence of the same consonant sounds at the beginning of words in close succession (e.g. 'ripe, red raspberry')
assonance The repetition of vowel sounds within words (e.g. rain, main)
metaphor A type of figurative language used to describe a person or object through an implicit comparison to something with similar characteristics
simile A device comparing 2 things that are not alike. Similes use 'like', 'as' or 'than' to make the comparison (e.g. The cake was as light as air)
metonymy A use of the name of one thing or attribute of something to represent something larger or related (e.g. using the word 'Crown' to represent a monarch of a country)

Additionally, aspects such as the structure and form of poems can enhance their aesthetic **style**. Poetic forms like sonnets, haikus and ballads conform to particular patterns of lines, syllables, stanzas and metres that contribute to their visual appearance on the page and their **purpose** of engaging the audience's senses, resulting in their aesthetic appeal. The precise, careful selection of powerful, connotative words is also a significant aesthetic feature of poetry.

style The distinctive language features, text structures and/or subject matter in a text which may shape meaning, be enjoyed for its aesthetic qualities or distinguish the work of an author, period etc.
purpose An intended or assumed reason for a type of text

2.7 Check for understanding

1 Carefully read the list of aesthetic qualities and their explanations previously outlined in the diagram.

2 Highlight any words in the explanations that are unfamiliar to you.

3 Compile a list of definitions for the unfamiliar words in the space provided.

____

____

____

____

Song lyrics

Song lyrics are much like poems, in that they also create an aesthetic experience through the deliberate use of language features like figurative devices, **imagery** and connotative words and **phrases**. Like poetry, song lyrics usually have a rhythmic quality, following a particular metre or structure and creating rhyme or repetition.

imagery Visually descriptive or figurative language to represent things including objects, actions and ideas in ways that appeal to the senses of the reader or viewer
phrase A group of words often beginning with a preposition but without a subject and verb combination (e.g. 'on the river'; 'with brown eyes')

'Took the Children Away', is a song written and performed by Uncle Archie Roach (8 January 1956 – 30 July 2022), an internationally famous Gunditjmara (Kirrae Whurrong/Djab Wurrung) and Bundjalung songwriter, singer and guitarist. Scan the QR code to listen to him singing the song. Search for the lyrics online to answer the following questions.

2.8 Check for understanding

1 'Took the Children Away' is written in the form of a ballad – a song that tells a story. Why do you think Uncle Archie Roach chose to tell the story in this way?

____

____

2 Who is the persona in these song lyrics?

____

3 How would you describe the voice of the persona? Try to provide some specific adjectives to describe the tone and personality of the voice.

4 Uncle Archie Roach uses a great deal of repetition in the lyrics. For example, one repeated image is that of the mother. How do the references to the mother increase the emotional impact of the song?

5 Discuss some effects that are achieved through other repeated words and images.

'Took the Children Away' tells the story of the children, like Uncle Archie Roach himself, who were removed from their families as a result of Australian government policy from the late 1800s until 1969. They are now referred to as the Stolen Generations. Therefore, the representations created by Uncle Archie Roach in his song reflect a certain historical Australian **context** that has had lasting impacts on First Nations people. Undertake some research about the Stolen Generations to enhance your understanding of the song.

context An environment or situation (social, cultural or historical) in which a text is responded to or created. Or wording surrounding an unfamiliar word, which a reader or listener uses to understand its meaning

2.9 Check for understanding

1 In the first verse of the song, who are 'they'? Why do you think this impersonal word has been selected by Uncle Archie Roach?

2 The **simile** 'like sheep' is used in the first verse of the song. Discuss what Uncle Archie Roach means by this.

______

______

______

3 The second verse (following the first chorus) describes the way in which First Nations people were betrayed by being promised a better life but treated badly. How does Uncle Archie Roach suggest that what the children learned was of little value to his people?

______

______

______

4 Uncle Archie Roach tells the story of his own removal in verse 3 (beginning 'One dark day on Framlingham'). Framlingham was Uncle Archie Roach's childhood home before he was put in an orphanage and then sent to several foster homes at a young age. How is language used in this verse to create a representation of his parents as powerless against the forces of the government?

______

______

______

5 Uncle Archie Roach spent years as an adult trying to find his family and using music and songs to express his anguish and loss. How does this song capture the extreme emotion of the children being taken from their families in the first four verses?

______

______

______

6 To what extent do you think Uncle Archie Roach adopts a fictional persona? Provide reasons for your answer with reference to your research and your biographical knowledge of Uncle Archie Roach.

______

______

7 In the final line of the fourth verse and the last two choruses, Uncle Archie Roach describes a happy homecoming. In reality, many children of the Stolen Generations lost their names, their languages, their families and their communities.

a Why do you think the song ends with a wistful tone?

b What emotions does the ending of the song evoke in you?

8 The full aesthetic appeal of the song is apparent in listening to it, rather than reading it. If you haven't already listened to Uncle Archie Roach's own rendition, access it now online and then explain how the sound of the music and the lyrics enhances its artistic qualities and stimulates a strong emotional response in listeners. Make sure you specify what these emotions are.

2.10 Get creative

1 In your English notebook, craft your own song lyrics that meet the following requirements:

a Select a real context to reflect upon in the lyrics, such as an historical event or an Australian location.

b Aim to represent the people, groups or places associated with your chosen context.

c Decide on a clear persona and voice for your lyrics.

d Use a range of aesthetic qualities to create an emotional impact.

Investigating feature articles

What issues are getting national or international attention right now? Think about some of the leading news stories that are generating conversation and varied opinions in society. Many contemporary stories explore issues related to food production. This unit examines examples of how food production has been explored in the media, as well as the conventions associated with feature articles.

In this unit, you will learn:

- to recognise the values communicated implicitly or explicitly in writing
- to identify the conventions of feature articles
- how publication contexts affect the structure of feature articles.
- to create your own feature articles.

Curriculum content

Australian Curriculum content description	Content code
Understand that language used to evaluate, implicitly or explicitly reveals an individual's values.	**AC9E10LA02**
Understand how paragraph structure can be varied to create cohesion, and paragraphs and images can be integrated for different purposes.	**AC9E10LA04**
Analyse and evaluate how authors organise ideas in texts to achieve a purpose.	**AC9E10LY04**

Issues

'Issues' are topics of public discussion and debate. The term can refer to concerns, challenges or problems related to a particular subject or topic that require improvement or resolution. Issues can be grouped in various categories such as social issues, environmental issues and economic issues.

3.1 Reflecting and discussing

Discuss the following questions in pairs, in small groups or with the whole class as directed by your teacher.

1 What issues are currently being debated in society which you have an opinion about?

2 What issues related to food production do you know about? Brainstorm a list of these issues.

3 Do you have any strong opinions about any of these issues? Explain why.

Feature articles

Feature articles are usually longer than news reports and use more varied and expressive language. They are more investigative in their **style** than news reports, which are objective in their reporting of the facts of a story. The writer of a feature article may use personal **pronouns** and include their own opinion about an issue. Like a news report, though, a feature article should answer six key questions about the topic:

what? who? where? when? why? how?

A feature article typically includes the following **conventions** to present a **perspective** on a topic.

style The distinctive language features, text structures and/or subject matter in a text which may shape meaning, be enjoyed for its aesthetic qualities or distinguish the work of an author, period etc.
pronoun A word that takes the place of a noun (e.g. I, me, he, she, herself, you, it, that, they, few, many, who, whoever, someone, everybody, and many others)
convention An accepted practice that has developed over time and is generally used and understood (e.g. use of punctuation)
perspective A lens through which the author perceives the world and creates a text, or the lens through which the reader or viewer perceives the world and understands a text

engaging and catchy headline, sometimes using a pun

byline naming the feature article's author

lead paragraph that introduces the topic or hooks the reader with an interesting anecdote or rhetorical question

subheadings to break up the text and provide a clear structure

engaging descriptive or figurative language, such as **metaphors**, **similes** and sensory **imagery**

evidence of research through statistics, case studies, facts and empirical data

quotations from experts, eyewitnesses or people related to the topic

varied paragraph and sentence lengths, but generally quite short paragraphs

balanced viewpoint that may consider various perspectives and opinions

metaphor A type of figurative language used to describe a person or object through an implicit comparison to something with similar characteristics
simile A device comparing 2 things that are not alike. Similes use 'like', 'as' or 'than' to make the comparison (e.g. The cake was as light as air)
imagery Visually descriptive or figurative language to represent things including objects, actions and ideas in ways that appeal to the senses of the reader or viewer

The following feature article is from the Melbourne newspaper *The Age*. It reports on a community garden in inner-suburban St Kilda.

An oasis of friendship grows with the veggies

by Michelle Hamer

While arty types sip lattes in nearby Acland Street cafes, Lenny Pastro is holding court on a bench outside Veg Out's communal kitchen.

'Just ask for Lenny when you get here, everyone knows me,' he assures me when I phone to organise the interview. After nine years as a plot holder he is an institution at Veg Out. The space has become his home and the other gardeners his second family.

Veg Out is a celebration of the suburban backyard, where rusty gates, bits of old timber and sheets of corrugated iron are reinvented as sculptures and fences. This was once a bowling green, and the faded metal lights still swing above the gardens on slack wires. The patch of land, preserved for permanent public use since 1881, is administered by the Bayside City Council.

There is a quirkiness and wry sense of humour expressed in the ironic garden statues; the gnomes and flamingoes, in the daggy mail boxes that announce each new plot, the totem pole artworks and bejewelled mosaic walls. There's no preciousness about this place, the vegetables, succulents, annuals and ground cover spill into other plots and communal areas. Although they are laid back, the 140 plot holders are passionate about their gardening. And there is a long waiting list for vacant plots.

It's a chaotic, messy, tangled, relaxed place to be, and for Lenny, it is an oasis of friendship and recreation.

Just past the pungent compost heap are Lenny's Girls – the chooks he cares for each day. Inside the weatherboard hen house is a new family of chicks that he is keeping an eye on. In Lenny's plot, which costs him about $150 a year to lease, potato plants jostle for position alongside herbs, tomatoes and other vegetables. He gives most of them away; he doesn't need much living alone in a small flat in Acland Street.

He has lived in St Kilda for 30 years now and loves the vibrancy of the place. He grew up on a commercial garden just out of Venice and after immigrating to Australia, he was variously employed at a milk factory, as a labourer, bricklayer and finally as a fork-lift driver for 26 years with Kraft at Port Melbourne. 'I was retrenched, I didn't retire,' he is at pains to explain.

A strong work ethic is ingrained in him; and being at the garden every day fulfils his need for activity and usefulness. 'I always worked hard, so what am I going to do now? Sit in my flat and watch the television? I'd rather be out here in the garden, there's always someone to talk to, something to do, I love it,' he says.

He is involved in all aspects of running the garden, from helping organise the monthly farmers' markets, to building an on-site pizza oven, giving other plot holders gardening tips and collecting broken bicycles and building new ones from their parts, which he gives to anyone who needs one.

His grandsons have been to visit his garden plot and spent time with him at Veg Out. 'They love it here, they can be in the fresh air and poke around. It's a good life,' he beams contentedly.

3.2 Check for understanding

1 Tick all of the feature article conventions listed here that are used in the text above.

a engaging headline ☐

b byline ☐

c lead paragraph that hooks the reader ☐

d subheadings ☐

e descriptive or figurative language ☐

f evidence of research ☐

g quotations ☐

h varied paragraph and sentence lengths ☐

i balanced viewpoint ☐

2 Identify the information presented in the article that addresses the 'what, who, where, when, why and how' questions of its main topic.

a What is the report about? ______________________________

b Who are the people concerned? ______________________________

c Where is the subject of the article located? ______________________________

d When does it take place? ______________________________

e Why has it developed? ______________________________

f How is it run? ______________________________

3 The community garden's name is Veg Out, which is a pun, or play on words. Provide some examples of other figurative devices or clever use of language apparent in the feature article.

____

____

____

____

____

4 What **adjectives** does the article's author use to show that the garden is unusual in its appearance?

____

____

adjective A word class that describes, identifies or quantifies a noun or a pronoun, e.g. two (number or quantity), my (possessive), ancient (descriptive), shorter (comparative), wooden (classifying)

Understanding tone

Although the **purposes** of a feature article are partly to convey information and to present a seemingly balanced account of a topic, in reality it will reveal the personal **values** of the writer. Sometimes, these values are explicitly stated, such as through a call to action, which might be positioned in the lead statement, subheading or concluding statement.

Often, though, the writer's values are communicated more subtly and implicitly through the **tone** of their writing. Tone is the attitude conveyed towards a certain topic or subject. It can suggest an evaluation or judgement of the topic. Writers of feature articles can support their evaluations and views in a number of ways, such as through statistics, research, logic, expert opinions, anecdotes, case studies and quotations.

purpose An intended or assumed reason for a type of text
values Ideas and beliefs specific to individuals and groups
tone The mood created by the language features used by an author and the way the text makes the reader feel

3.3 Check for understanding

1 Based on the descriptions provided in paragraphs 4 and 5 of the feature article, what qualities of the garden do you think the writer values?

____

____

2 Circle the adjectives below that best describe the tone of the article.

admiring	warm	disapproving
approving	cynical	mocking

3 Identify some of the words and **phrases** in the article that contribute to its tone.

____

____

____

4 Although the writer does not explicitly state her evaluation of the garden's worth, her tone makes her attitude towards the garden apparent. What sort of evidence does she use to support her view?

____

____

5 Two paragraphs in the article are only one sentence long. What is the effect of these very short paragraphs on the reader?

____

____

6 Why do you think the author quotes Lenny directly?

____

____

phrase A group of words often beginning with a preposition but without a subject and verb combination (e.g. 'on the river'; 'with brown eyes')

Images

Feature articles frequently contain integrated images that are used for a range of purposes, such as to:

- generate reader interest or grab their attention
- support or illustrate a point made or an idea raised in the written text of the article
- provoke thoughts or ideas in the minds of readers.

The following image was used to open a feature article titled 'Is This the Future of Food?' written by Jenne Brammer and published both online and in the broadsheet newspaper version of *The West Australian* on 29 August 2021.

SUNDAY, AUGUST 29, 2021 NEWS 15

IS THIS THE FUTURE OF FOOD?

SPECIAL!

A 3D burger, a bowl of oat noodles and cricket tacos all washed down with a nice camel milk latte – it may sound a bit strange, but it's all part of the increasing appetite for sustainable and nutritious cuisine, writes Jenne Brammer

"Hello and welcome to the future of food. Can I take your order?"

"Yes, I'll have a 3D-printed burger with a side of crickets and a camel milk shake please. Oh, and give me one of those mealworm muesli bars for later."

Such a transaction at the local takeaway or fast food joint would have been inconceivable not so long ago. It still sounds weird, but maybe not for much longer.

There's a revolution bubbling away in the food industry. Everything from what we eat, how it is produced, down to the very definition of food, seems about to be turned on its head.

Environmental concerns, population growth, advanced technology, health consciousness and evolving ethical considerations are the ingredients fermenting change.

Thrown into the same pot, they're being stirred together by time and circumstance, and the result is a strange stew indeed. Insects, plant-based meat, camel milk, lupins and vegetables grown in towers – all are among vanguard of the "foods of the future" as consumers change their diets in pursuit of sustainability and health.

The UN's Intergovernmental Panel on Climate Change's recent warning that the world is warming more quickly than initially thought is only expected to accelerate changing food consumption habits.

Chris Vas, general manager of the WA Food Innovation precinct at Peel, said the warming climate and limited resources was driving change.

"Globally there is more attention being paid to the environmental footprint and sustainability issues, given the increasing population and scarce natural resources such as water," he said.

Red meat consumption is declining

Continued P16

3.4 Check for understanding

1 How does the image work to capture the attention of readers?

____

____

2 How does the image relate to the written text provided by supporting its main idea?

____

____

3 What visual effect is created by the typography of the article's headline, made to look like a butcher's blackboard?

____

____

4 What idea is conveyed by labelling different parts of the illustrated cricket?

____

____

5 What issues related to food production do you think the article will explore?

____

____

Read the opening of the feature article 'Is This the Future of Food?', which has been reproduced below.

'Hello and welcome to the future of food. Can I take your order?'

'Yes, I'll have a 3D-printed burger with a side of crickets and a camel milk shake please. Oh, and give me one of those mealworm muesli bars for later.'

Such a transaction at the local takeaway or fast food joint would have been inconceivable not so long ago. It still sounds weird, but maybe not for much longer.

There's a revolution bubbling away in the food industry. Everything from what we eat, how it is produced, down to the very definition of food, seems about to be turned on its head.

Environmental concerns, population growth, advanced technology, health consciousness and evolving ethical considerations are the ingredients fermenting change.

Thrown into the same pot, they're being stirred together by time and circumstance, and the result is a strange stew indeed. Insects, plant-based meat, camel milk, lupins and vegetables grown in towers — all are among vanguard of the 'foods of the future' as consumers change their diets in pursuit of sustainability and health.

The UN's Intergovernmental Panel on Climate Change's recent warning that the world is warming more quickly than initially thought is only expected to accelerate changing food consumption habits.

Chris Vas, general manager of the WA Food Innovation precinct at Peel, said the warming climate and limited resources was driving change.

'Globally there is more attention being paid to the environmental footprint and sustainability issues, given the increasing population and scarce natural resources such as water,' he said.

Red meat consumption is declining despite the desire for protein rich diets. By 2027 the amount of red meat eaten by Australians annually is projected to drop from 25 kg to 21 kg per capita.

Worldwide, companies are furiously developing alternatives. They include meat and seafood in labs grown from stem cells from cattle and fish and produced by a 3D printer. Then there's those already carving out a niche in supermarkets with plant-based meat products. Another company has produced a prawn made out of soy protein and algae.

And there has been major investment, including in Australia, in insect farming, which aims to replace carbon-intensive protein from cattle, sheep and pigs with low-impact crickets and worms.

Biotechnology expert Dr Simon Carroll, chairman of the WA co-ordinating committee for National Science Week, said it takes about 37,000 litres of water to create 1 kg of beef.

3.5

Check for understanding

1 What do you notice about the lengths of the paragraphs in the feature article?

2 What feature article conventions are included in this extract?

3 How is the opening of the feature article written to hook the reader's attention?

4 What food- or cooking-related references and puns are made by the author throughout paragraphs 4–6 of the article?

5 What reasons are provided in the extract for the changes being made to the types of foods produced and the practices used to make foods?

6 What do you think is the author's opinion about the topic of the article? Provide reasons for your answer.

Reading paths and publication contexts

The path that our eyes follow when reading something online is different from the path followed when we read it in hard copy (print) in a book or newspaper.

When we read something online, our eyes travel vertically down the screen as we scroll, but we typically read from left to right on a printed page. The content of feature articles in printed newspapers or magazines is often structured in two columns, whereas the online version of the same content is usually in one column centred on the screen, often with pop-ups and advertising in the margins.

3.6 Reflecting and discussing

Discuss the following questions in pairs, in small groups or with the whole class as directed by your teacher.

1 What sorts of texts do you usually read online?

2 How do you access this reading material? Is it on a mobile phone, a desktop computer or something else?

3 What kinds of texts do you usually read in hard copy?

4 In what different **contexts** do you read texts online and in printed versions? For example, do you read them at home or on public transport? When you're killing time or relaxing?

5 Do you prefer reading digital or printed texts? Provide reasons for your answer.

6 What reading paths are followed in some other languages?

context An environment or situation (social, cultural or historical) in which a text is responded to or created. Or wording surrounding an unfamiliar word, which a reader or listener uses to understand its meaning

3.7 Get creative

1 Select a topic related to one of the broad subjects of food production.

a food security and scarcity

b genetically modified food

c fast-food impacts on human health

d sustainability

e food wastage

f food labelling and transparency

g impacts of global warming on food production

2 In your English notebook, compile research notes that focus on the 'what, who, where, when, why and how' questions connected with your topic. Record evidence to support your understanding of the issue.

3 Identify the purpose and target audience of your feature article.

____

____

4 Keeping the purpose and audience of your feature article in mind, identify the type of publication your feature article would suit and whether it would be most appropriate in a print or digital format.

____

5 Draft your feature article in your English notebook, ensuring that you use all of the feature article conventions listed earlier in this unit.

6 Carefully **edit** your article for expression, grammar, spelling and punctuation.

edit To prepare, alter, adapt or refine with attention to grammar, spelling, punctuation and vocabulary

Novel study: *Animal Farm*

A great book can immerse us in other worlds, expose us to interesting or unfamiliar experiences and generate the full spectrum of human emotions.

This unit will guide you through the study of a well-known and highly regarded piece of literature, George Orwell's novel *Animal Farm*. You will be helped to understand and explore this literary classic as an allegorical political satire.

In this unit, you will learn:

- to express interpretations and responses to literature such as novels
- to recognise the representation of people, places, events and concepts in texts
- how literary texts can reflect real historical, social and cultural contexts.

Curriculum content

Australian Curriculum content description	Content code
Reflect on and extend others' interpretations of and responses to literature.	AC9E10LE02
Evaluate the social, moral or ethical positions represented in literature.	AC9E10LE04
Analyse how text structure, language features, literary devices and intertextual connections shape interpretations of texts.	AC9E10LE05
Analyse and evaluate how people, places, events and concepts are represented in texts and reflect contexts.	AC9E10LY01

Synopsis

George Orwell's short novel *Animal Farm*, first published in 1945, is a modern political fable. It is technically considered a novella due to its brevity. The book tells the story of a group of farmyard animals who revolt against their cruel and neglectful owner, farmer Mr Jones, and set up a system in which they run the farm for themselves. It begins as a hopeful dream and an opportunity for equality, but over time, divisions grow between the animals. Eventually, the pigs – the most intelligent animals – take power for themselves. Their privilege and wealth are protected by vicious dogs that the pigs have trained since they were pups.

4.1 Reflecting and discussing

Discuss the following questions in pairs, in small groups or with the whole class as directed by your teacher.

1 Have you heard of the novel *Animal Farm* before?

2 What are your expectations of the novel's genre, characters, plot and setting based on the front cover image reproduced at the beginning of the unit?

3 What are your expectations of the novel's genre, characters, plot and setting based on its title?

4 The original title of the book was *Animal Farm: A Fairy Story*. How does the addition of this subtitle change or strengthen your expectations of its content?

Vocabulary

Understanding and analysing *Animal Farm* is far easier if you have a bank of useful words to draw from and apply to the text. Using precise terminology will help you to demonstrate an understanding of the text's genre, construction and themes.

4.2 Check for understanding

Provide definitions for the following terms, which can be used in the analysis of *Animal Farm*.

Term	Definition
novella	
allegory	
fable	

Term	Definition
satire	
anthropomorphism	
Marxism	
Communism	
revolution	
totalitarianism	
propaganda	
maxim	
Bolshevik	

The extract from the novel below occurs when the farm's two dominant pigs, Napoleon and Snowball, gather the animals to vote on whether to build a windmill on the farm.

> [Napoleon] said very quietly that the windmill was nonsense and that he advised nobody to vote for it, and promptly sat down again; he had spoken for barely thirty seconds, and seemed almost indifferent as to the effect he produced. At this Snowball sprang to his feet, and … broke into a passionate appeal in favour of the windmill. Until now the animals had been about equally divided in their sympathies, but in a moment Snowball's eloquence had carried them away. In glowing sentences he painted a picture of Animal Farm as it might be when sordid labour was lifted from the animals' backs … Electricity, he said, could operate threshing machines, ploughs, harrows, rollers, and reapers and binders, besides supplying every stall with its own electric light, hot and cold water, and an electric heater. By the time he had finished speaking, there was no doubt as to which way the vote would go. But just at this moment Napoleon stood up and, casting a peculiar sidelong look at Snowball, uttered a high-pitched whimper of a kind no one had ever heard him utter before.

At this there was a terrible baying sound outside, and nine enormous dogs wearing brass-studded collars came bounding into the barn. They dashed straight for Snowball, who only sprang from his place just in time to escape their snapping jaws. In a moment he was out of the door and they were after him. Too amazed and frightened to speak, all the animals crowded through the door to watch the chase.

4.3

Check for understanding

1 Napoleon and Snowball have been equal leaders of the revolution until this point. What is Snowball's great talent which temporarily places him in a position of superiority?

____

____

2 What real group from history do the 'enormous dogs wearing brass-studded collars' represent? You may need to conduct some research.

____

____

3 What is the reaction of the other animals to the dogs chasing Snowball?

____

____

The novel later describes the events that follow Snowball's expulsion from the farm.

Napoleon, with the dogs following him, now mounted onto the raised portion of the floor where Major had previously stood to deliver his speech. He announced that from now on, the Sunday-morning Meetings would come to an end. They were unnecessary, he said, and wasted time. In future all questions relating to the working of the farm would be settled by a special committee of pigs, presided over by himself. These would meet in private and afterwards communicate the decisions to others. The animals would still assemble on Sunday mornings to salute the flag, sing 'Beasts of England', and receive their orders for the week; but there would be no more debates.

4.4 Check for understanding

1 How does this new decision-making process mark a shift in the leadership of the farm?

2 What do you think is the purpose of bringing the animals together weekly to sing 'Beasts of England'?

> Afterwards Squealer was sent round the farm to explain the new arrangement to the others.
>
> 'Comrades,' he said, 'I trust that every animal here appreciates the sacrifice that Comrade Napoleon has made in taking this extra labour upon himself. Do not imagine, comrades, that leadership is a pleasure! On the contrary, it is a deep and heavy responsibility. No one believes more firmly than Comrade Napoleon that all animals are equal.'

3 What kind of leader does Squealer represent Napoleon to be in his explanation?

4 The animals refer to each other as 'comrades'. What does this term imply?

5 What examples of irony are evident in Squealer's explanation to the other animals?

Representations of people, places, events and concepts

Animal Farm is widely perceived as an allegory of the 1917 Russian Revolution. The actions and events of the text closely parallel those of this revolution and the people involved.

4.5 Check for understanding

Make research notes on the following important events, concepts and political figures that are represented allegorically in *Animal Farm*.

Historical events and political figures	Research notes	Parallels in *Animal Farm*
Tsar Nicholas II		Mr Jones
Vladimir Lenin and Karl Marx		Old Major
Communism		Animalism
Leon Trotsky		Snowball
Joseph Stalin		Napoleon
Stalin's Five-Year Plan		building of the windmill
October Revolution		Battle of the Cowshed
Soviet Union flag		Animal Farm flag
Heaven/Paradise		Sugarcandy Mountain

More than just representing the Russian Revolution, *Animal Farm* can also be read as a work of satirical social commentary on humanity and on the abuse of power more generally. *Animal Farm* is also a product of its World War II era, during which the public became more aware of government influences and political threats.

In addition, the novel continues to serve as a warning about the dangers and dire consequences of power being exploited by a privileged few in other **contexts**. One of the ways in which it achieves this is by using animal characters rather than specific people. The animals can be seen to represent certain groups, collective identities and types of people in society generally.

context An environment or situation (social, cultural or historical) in which a text is responded to or created. Or wording surrounding an unfamiliar word, which a reader or listener uses to understand its meaning

4.6 Check for understanding

During or after reading the novel, answer these questions.

1 What kind of personality traits and **values** does Mollie possess?

____

2 Does Mollie remind you of certain groups or types of people in contemporary society? If so, who?

____

____

3 What personal quality does Boxer possess that enables him to be exploited? Circle the correct answer below.

sense of humour | friendly demeanour | strong work ethic

kindness | empathy with others

4 What personal qualities do the pigs possess that enable them to become the new leaders of the farm?

____

____

5 The hens face many challenges and make any sacrifices on *Animal Farm*. What group of people in society might they represent?

____

____

values Ideas and beliefs specific to individuals and groups

6 How do the sheep demonstrate their blind obedience to authority?

7 Explain the significance of Benjamin in the story.

8 Circle the **adjectives** below that best describe the ducks and geese.

aggressive passive defiant accepting

resistant cynical suspicious

9 What does the cat symbolise in *Animal Farm*?

10 Do you think the relationship between the animals on the farm successfully represents a microcosm (a small-scale version) of real society? Provide reasons for your answer.

adjective A word class that describes, identifies or quantifies a noun or a pronoun, e.g. two (number or quantity), my (possessive), ancient (descriptive), shorter (comparative), wooden (classifying)

Moral and ethical positions

Animal Farm is a fable because it contains a clear moral (main lesson or message) delivered through a story involving animal characters. Fables function as instruments for teaching readers valuable lessons through their morals.

4.7 Reflecting and discussing

Discuss the following questions in pairs, in small groups or with the whole class as directed by your teacher.

1 What do you believe is the moral of *Animal Farm*?

2 Do you think *Animal Farm* would have been as successful if it were not a fable about animals but had human characters instead?

3 What other fables do you know and what morals do they communicate?

The morals contained in literature usually reveal the ethical position of the author on certain topics. You can probably identify – through the moral messages of *Animal Farm* – that George Orwell didn't think very highly of political systems that oppress the masses and give power to only an elite few! The novel suggests that he believed the actions of some political leaders to be unethical – morally wrong and unjust. Orwell's ethical position, evident not only in *Animal Farm* but in his other great works such as *1984*, was probably shaped by values such as equality, justice and freedom of speech.

4.8 Get creative

1 Fables use animal characters to give a moral or lesson. Go online to find some of Aesop's fables.

2 In a fable, animal characters are used to represent human qualities. Brainstorm human characteristics that the following animals could represent. Try to think beyond the first, most obvious characteristic and include other appropriate ideas.

owl	
crow	
dog	
lion	
mouse	

3 Using some of the animals above and your ethical position on a topic, develop an idea for your own short fable. What will the moral of your fable be?

____

____

4 In your English notebook, draft your short fable.

Language, propaganda and power

In *Animal Farm*, the pigs use slogans or maxims (short, punchy **phrases**) as a means of propaganda to manipulate ideas. 'Four legs good, two legs bad' soon becomes 'Four legs good, two legs better' as the pigs teach themselves to walk upright. 'All animals are equal' changes by the end of the novel to 'All animals are equal but some are more equal than others.'

phrase A group of words often beginning with a preposition but without a subject and verb combination (e.g. 'on the river'; 'with brown eyes')

4.9

Check for understanding

1 How do the maxims above suggest a power imbalance between the animals?

____

____

2 What other maxims in the novel reveal a hierarchy of power through language?

____

____

3 Find the origins of the following slogans and explain the message that each one was intended to convey.

a 'Arbeit macht frei.'

____

____

b 'The buck stops here.'

____

____

c 'Workers of the world, unite!'

____

____

As demonstrated in *Animal Farm*, those who control language can exert power and influence over others, effectively using that language to disempower.

4.10 Reflecting and discussing

Discuss the following questions in pairs, in small groups or with the whole class as directed by your teacher.

1 What are some examples of people using language to empower or disempower people in contemporary Australian society?

2 What are the implications of artificial intelligence language models for social power and control?

Interpretations and responses

The allegorical fable form of *Animal Farm*, with its anthropomorphic characters and **intertextual references** to other political satires, results in some interesting interpretations and responses. The word 'interpretation' refers to the meaning we make from a text, regarding its ideas, **themes** and **purposes**.

Interpretations of texts can be widely varied and not always in keeping with the intentions of an author. For instance, *Animal Farm* was rejected by one publisher because they thought it was a children's book that wouldn't sell! Below are three interpretations of *Animal Farm*.

intertextual references Associations or connections between one text and other texts that may be overt or less explicit. They can take the form of direct quotation, parody, allusion or structural borrowing
theme The main idea, concept or message of a text
purpose An intended or assumed reason for a type of text

- Interpretation 1: *Animal Farm* serves as a powerful critique of the abuse of power, illustrating how revolutionary ideals can be distorted and exploited by those in authority.
- Interpretation 2: *Animal Farm* portrays the Russian Revolution and the rise of Stalin through a fable about farm animals, revealing the corrupting nature of power and the betrayal of ideals.
- Interpretation 3: *Animal Farm* serves as a cautionary tale about the dangers of totalitarianism, highlighting the manipulation and oppression of the masses in pursuit of absolute control.

4.11 Check for understanding

1 Which of these three interpretations of *Animal Farm* most closely resembles the meaning you take from the text? Explain why.

____

____

____

2 Extend the interpretation you have chosen by adding one or two more sentences that elaborate on the meaning it makes from the novel.

____

____

____

3 Think of one more possible interpretation of the text and write it below as a full sentence.

____

____

____

4 Do you think *Animal Farm* could be interpreted as a children's book? Explain your answer.

____

____

'Responses' are the reactions we have to a text, including what or how it makes us think, feel or act. Responses can therefore be emotional, intellectual or physical.

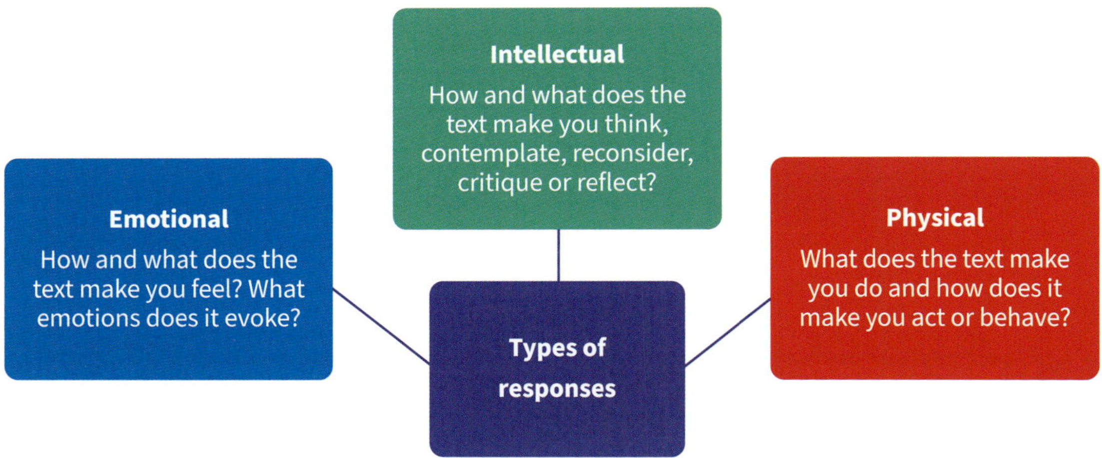

Of course, we respond differently to different parts of a text. We may respond with disgust towards one character and with sympathy for another; we may respond with interest and curiosity to one part of the plot and with criticism to another. We can also experience intellectual, emotional and physical responses all at the same time. Try to articulate exactly what aspect you are reacting to when detailing your response to a text.

4.12

Check for understanding

Do you consider the following responses to be emotional, intellectual or physical? Write your answers in the space provided.

Animal Farm left me feeling a mixture of anger and frustration at the betrayal of the animals. ________________

Animal Farm made me think about the corrupting influence of power and the manipulation of language for political control. ________________

The ending of *Animal Farm*, highlighting the cyclical nature of oppression, left me with a sense of despair. ________________

The intense confrontations and conflicts in *Animal Farm* made my heart race.

____

I felt a deep sense of sympathy and compassion for the animals during their struggle against the pigs' tyranny. ________________

I found *Animal Farm* intellectually engaging, provoking thoughts about social hierarchies, revolutions and the nature of leadership. ________________

I literally teared up during the description of Boxer's final moments; it was so heartbreaking! ________________

4.13

Reflecting and discussing

Discuss the following questions in pairs, in small groups or with the whole class as directed by your teacher.

1 Share some of your personal interpretations of and responses to *Animal Farm*.

2 Find some online reviews of *Animal Farm* that contain new or interesting interpretations of and responses to the novel. Do any of the interpretations or responses cause you to think about the text differently or more deeply?

UNIT 5

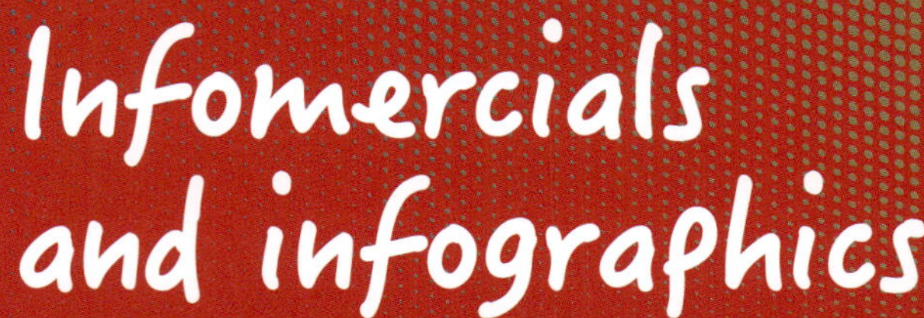

Infomercials and infographics

Texts that combine written text and visual images are an integral part of our daily lives. This unit will help you to examine and create such multimodal texts, with a particular focus on poster-form infomercials and infographics. The important features of these non-fiction informational texts will be explored.

In this unit, you will learn:

- about the common features of infomercials and infographics
- how the features of still and moving images create representations
- to create your own multimodal texts for a specific audience and purpose.

Curriculum content

Australian Curriculum content description	Content code
Evaluate the features of still and moving images, and the effects of those choices on representations.	AC9E10LA07
Plan, create, edit and publish written and multimodal texts, organising, expanding and developing ideas through experimenting with text structures, language features, literary devices and multimodal features for specific purposes and audiences in ways that may be imaginative, reflective, informative, persuasive, analytical and/or critical.	AC9E10LY06

Infomercials

The word 'infomercial' is a blend of 'information' and 'commercial'. It emerged in the 1980s to describe a type of television advertising that provides information about a product while still functioning as a commercial. Infomercials aim to persuade viewers to buy products by using exaggerated claims, user demonstrations and limited-time offers. They often air during breakfast or morning television, late at night or on specialised home-shopping channels.

5.1 Reflecting and discussing

Discuss the following questions in pairs, in small groups or with the whole class as directed by your teacher.

1 Brainstorm examples that combine written and visual elements to communicate information.

2 Where are these texts typically published or seen and read?

3 Why do you think texts that represent their ideas through a combination of visual and written elements can be so engaging?

Advertising features and techniques

Infomercials use recognisable advertising features and techniques to sell their products and ideas.

5.2 Check for understanding

1 Find an example of an infomercial on television or online and answer the following questions.

a What product is the infomercial advertising? ______________________

b Which of the advertising features and techniques listed in the following table are used in the infomercial?

____

____

c Who do you think is the target audience of the infomercial? Give reasons for your answer.

____

____

2 Draw lines to match the following common advertising features and techniques with their definitions.

Feature/technique	Definition
demonstration	using visuals such as charts, diagrams and infographics to convey information, statistics or comparisons in a visually engaging and easy-to-understand manner
informative graphics	comparing a problem or situation before using the product with the improved results after using the product, to emphasise the product's transformative potential
call-outs and captions	emphasising time-limited offers, discounts or bonuses to create a sense of urgency and encourage immediate action
before-and-after scenarios	showing the effectiveness or functionality of the product through live demonstrations or visual representations to provide proof of its capabilities
attention-grabbing headlines	presenting objective and verifiable information based on evidence that can be proved
testimonials and success stories	using bold and captivating titles to quickly capture the viewer's attention and spark their interest
limited-time offers and deals	including text call-outs and captions on an infomercial poster to highlight key features and benefits of the product
guarantees or warranties	featuring quotations from satisfied customers or celebrities who have experienced positive results or benefits from using the product
repetition and reinforcement	identifying a common problem or need and presenting the product as the ideal solution to address that problem effectively
close-up shots	assuring customers of the quality or effectiveness of the product by offering guarantees, warranties or money-back guarantees
problem–solution approach	repeating key messages, benefits or offers throughout the infomercial or infomercial poster to reinforce the product's value and make it stick in the viewer's memory
facts	presenting numerical data in the form of percentages, averages, graphs, charts etc.
statistics	utilising zoomed-in visuals to highlight specific product details or demonstrate the product's effectiveness in a more focused manner

The infomercial poster form

An infomercial poster is a type of advertising that uses still visuals to convey a message. Infomercial posters can be instrumental in sharing information about a business, product or industry with a target audience by using eye-catching graphics and clear written text. They are used to sell not just products, but messages too, particularly messages of social interest.

An infomercial poster typically comprises facts, statistics, graphics, charts and illustrations. It invites audiences to **skim** and **scan** for the most important information, rather than spend a long time reading lots of written text.

skim Reading quickly, selecting key words and details through a text to determine the general meaning or main messages or ideas

scan To read moving one's eyes quickly down a page seeking specific words and phrases. It is also used when a reader first finds information to determine whether it will answer their questions

5.3 Check for understanding

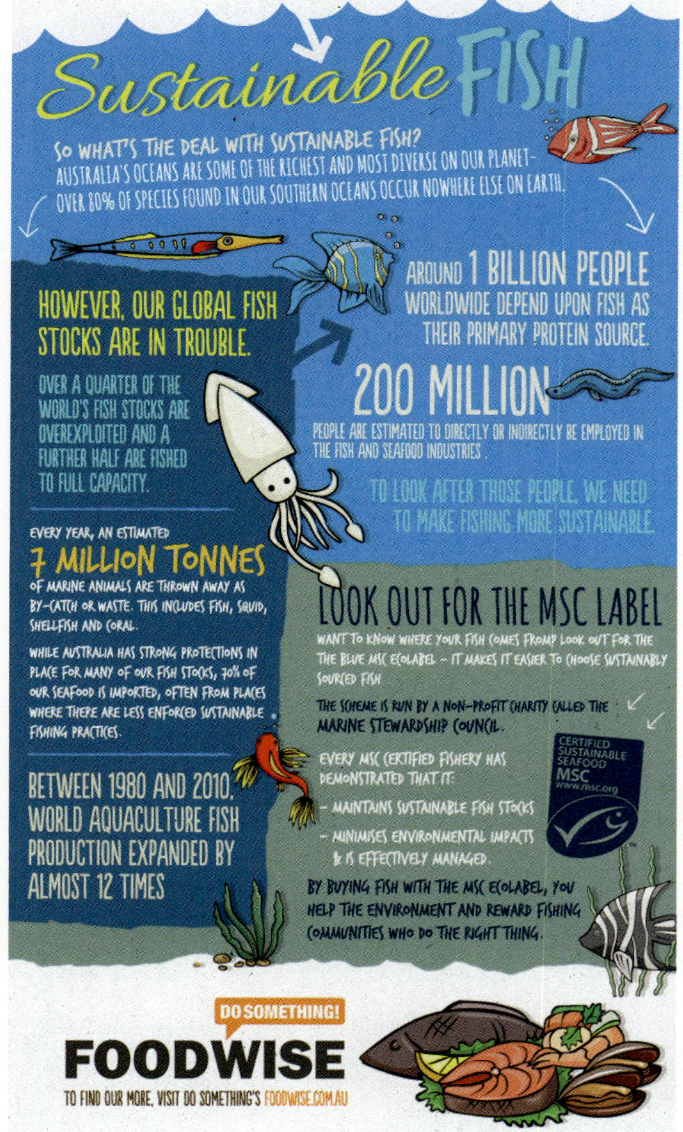

1 What product or brand is being advertised by this infomercial poster?

2 Who is the product or brand being promoted by?

3 Provide two examples of statistics from the infomercial poster.

4 Provide two examples of facts from the infomercial poster.

5 How would you describe the images in the infomercial poster? Circle the applicable options below.

realistic	representational	simple	eye-catching
photographic	concise	lifelike	naturalistic

6 As well as advertising a product, do you think the infomercial poster is convincing in promoting a message, too? Give reasons for your answer.

5.4 Get creative

1 Select one of the products below to design an infomercial poster for.

a an energy-boosting snack bar

b an eco-friendly water bottle

c a smart study desk

d an ergonomic backpack

e a mindful meditation app

2 Who will be the target audience for your infomercial poster? Why is this group an appropriate target market?

3 What advertisement and persuasive text **conventions** will you include in your infomercial to make it convincing?

____

____

4 Plan or design your infomercial poster in the space below.

convention An accepted practice that has developed over time and is generally used and understood (e.g. use of punctuation)

The magazine infomercial below blends information about new pet products with an eye-catching headline, a customer testimonial and photo demonstrations.

5.5 Check for understanding

1 The 'Sustainable Fish' and 'Pampered Pets' infomercials are very different in their construction and target audiences. Complete the following comparison table by describing each of the aspects identified in the left-hand column.

Features/ techniques	'Sustainable Fish'	'Pampered Pets'
Types of images		
Persuasive devices		
Target audience		

2 Which of the two infomercials is the most persuasive for you personally? Give reasons for your answer.

______

______

______

3 The infomercial 'Pampered Pets' uses **alliteration**. List all of the examples you can find. Why might this make the text more appealing or memorable?

______

______

______

4 The infomercial uses informal language. List four examples of this below.

______ ______

______ ______

5 How does the informal language contribute to the **tone** of the text?

______

______

6 The infomercial includes a customer testimonial. What do you think this adds to the infomercial's persuasive effect on readers?

______

______

______

7 How do the photographs of the dogs add to the infomercial's appeal?

______

______

______

8 Think about the infomercial's text design. Consider the typefaces and colours used for the headline and the body text. What do they suggest about the infomercial's target audience?

______

______

______

alliteration A recurrence of the same consonant sounds at the beginning of words in close succession (e.g. 'ripe, red raspberry')
phrase A group of words often beginning with a preposition but without a subject and verb combination (e.g. 'on the river'; 'with brown eyes')

Infographics

An infographic combines brief written information with graphics. Unlike infomercials, the **purpose** of an infographic is primarily to convey information clearly and quickly in bite-sized pieces rather than to persuade an audience.

An infographic's visual representation of information, through key facts, statistics, images, diagrams, charts, graphs and other visual elements, makes it easier to understand. These texts often select and summarise complex information in a succinct, reader-friendly manner. Look closely at the three examples of infographics below.

purpose An intended or assumed reason for a type of text

EXAMPLE A

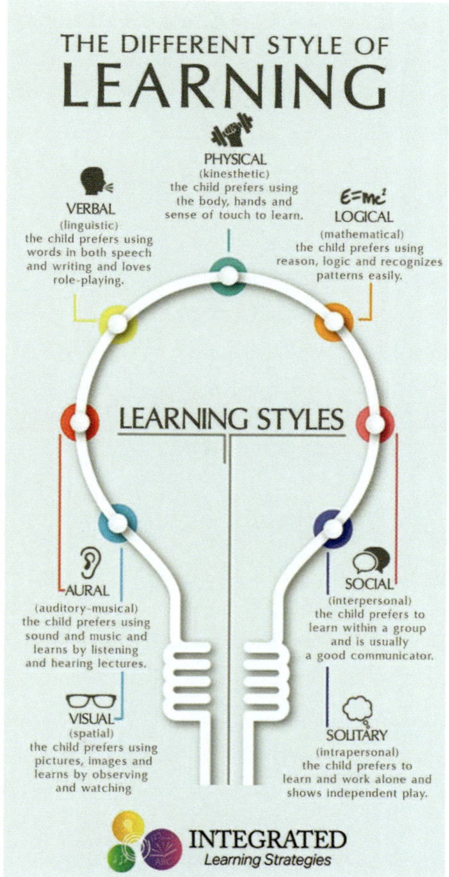

EXAMPLE B

EXAMPLE C

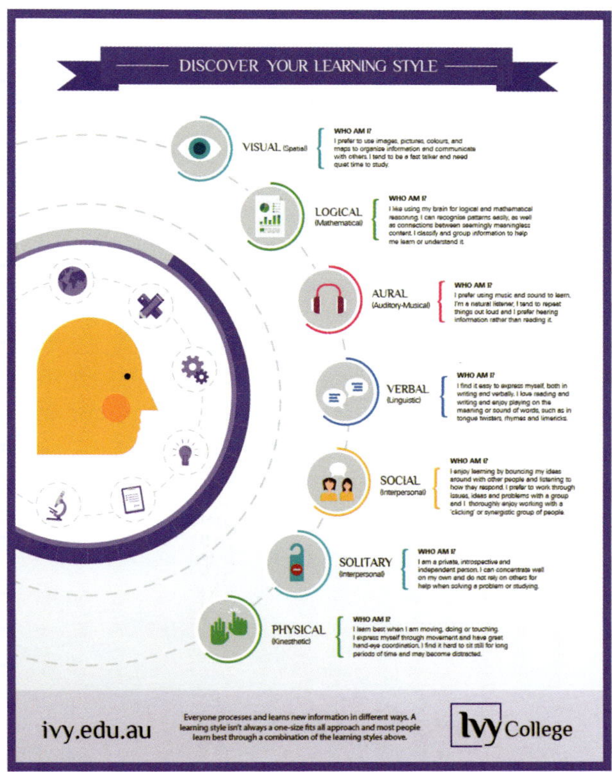

5.6 Check for understanding

1 What topic do all of these infographics have in common?

---

2 What infographic features does Example A include? Circle the correct options below.

icons	key facts	charts	statistics
images	graphs	diagrams	

3 What infographic features does Example B include? Circle the correct options below.

icons	key facts	charts	statistics
images	graphs	diagrams	

4 What infographic features does Example C include? Circle the correct options below.

icons	key facts	charts	statistics
images	graphs	diagrams	

5 Which of the infographics do you think includes the most appropriate images to represent its text? Give reasons for your answer.

---

6 Which of the infographics do you find the most visually engaging? Give reasons for your answer.

---

7 Annotate each of the infographics to indicate the reading pathways you take. Which of the infographics do you find the easiest to follow and understand? Give reasons for your answer.

---

8 What other types of texts are designed to convey information to the **audience** as their primary purpose?

____

____

9 Do you think infographics are more effective or less effective at communicating information than these other types of informative texts? Give reasons for your answer.

____

____

audience An intended or assumed group of readers, listeners or viewers that a writer, designer, filmmaker or speaker is addressing

5.7 Get creative

1 Select a topic that you are interested in or know a lot of information about related to one of the subjects below and write it the space provided.

a a sport or hobby ______________________________

b a specialist area of interest ______________________________

c an historical event ______________________________

d a significant person ______________________________

e a place or location. ______________________________

2 Now plan an infographic in your English notebook that communicates important information on this topic in a clear and engaging way. You may need to conduct some further research on your selected topic before starting.

3 Use a digital tool or program to create the final version of your infographic.

UNIT 6

Social issues on the stage

While theatre can be an exciting and entertaining experience, many playwrights use their works to make powerful comments about society. Topical issues, ongoing injustices and social inequalities are all subjects explored in many contemporary plays. Such plays seek to encourage conversations and offer the playwright's perspective on the world. Part of the power of theatre comes from being in the same room as real people as they bring to life – sometimes provocatively – the issues that concern our society.

In this unit, you will learn:

- about the functions of stage directions and dialogue
- how plays reflect the issues of their contexts
- how to write a monologue.

Curriculum content

Australian Curriculum content description	Content code
Analyse representations of individuals, groups and places and evaluate how they reflect their context in literary texts by First Nations Australian, and wide-ranging Australian and world authors.	AC9E10LE01
Evaluate the social, moral or ethical positions represented in literature.	AC9E10LE04
Create and edit literary texts with a sustained 'voice', selecting and adapting text structures, literary devices, and language, auditory and visual features for purposes and audiences.	AC9E10LE08
Plan, create, rehearse and deliver spoken and multimodal presentations by experimenting with rhetorical devices, and the organisation and development of ideas, to engage audiences for different purposes in ways that may be imaginative, reflective, informative, persuasive, analytical and/or critical.	AC9E10LY07

Play scripts

Play scripts are composed primarily of two elements: *stage directions* and *dialogue*. Accompanying these might be other features, such as a list of characters at the beginning of the play and descriptions of settings at the beginning of scenes. Sometimes, plays will have descriptions of the set design as well, referring to the specific elements involved in depicting the setting on stage.

Stage directions

When studying a play, you need to observe how the stage directions operate as the essential instructions that breathe life into the play's performance. Stage directions can range from detailed instructions articulating the playwright's vision for the play's performance to more sparse directions that allow the director and actors more scope to interpret the script.

Stage directions typically include the following elements.

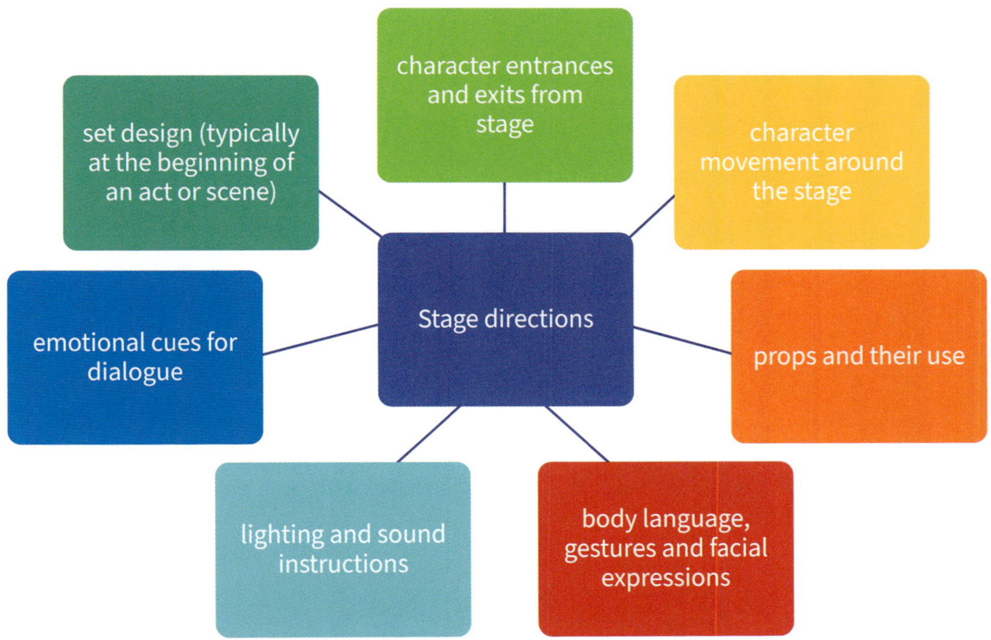

Rainbow's End, by playwright Jane Harrison, a descendant of the Muruwari people, is set in 1950s Australia on the river flats between Shepparton and Mooroopna in Victoria. Known as Rumbalara, or more colloquially as 'the Flats', this was a Yorta Yorta settlement founded after the Cummeragunja Walk Off in 1939, in which many families left the Cummeragunja Mission Station in protest against the terrible living conditions, exploitation of Yorta Yorta workers and poor management of the reserve.

Through the eyes of three generations of women, Harrison dramatises the Yorta Yorta people's struggle for recognition, equality and acceptance against the backdrop of Queen Elizabeth II's official visit to Australia in 1954.

1950s. A humpy on the riverbank. Clean and homely.

SCENE ONE (A)

Humpy interior. Morning. GLADYS is getting dressed up and humming to herself. DOLLY has her head down over her schoolbooks.

GLADYS listens in rapt silence to the voice of Queen Elizabeth II on the radio.

RADIO: [voice-over] ... standing at last on Australian soil, on this spot, which is the birthplace of the nation, I want to tell you all, how happy I am to be amongst you, and how much I look forward to my journey through Australia ...

The radio fades out as NAN enters.

GLADYS: That valve ... Where's my white gloves?

NAN DEAR: Gloves? Don't need white gloves to pick beans.

GLADYS doesn't react.

You're going into town then, for all that hullabaloo. Think of inviting me?

GLADYS: You? I know how you feel about royalty. Even if she is the 'first reigning monarch to visit our shores'.

DOLLY: Nan, I need your help with this.

She is doing homework.

NAN DEAR: One loyal subject in the family is enough. And someone's got to pick.

DOLLY: I'm doing our family tree.

NAN DEAR: Tree?

GLADYS: Don't know about loyal. Just going for a squiz.

NAN DEAR: Don't know where you get these ideas from sometimes.

GLADYS: I'm not hurting anyone, am I? It's a moment I'll remember ... to see our pretty young monarch and the Duke. I'm not going to miss it for all the tea in China!

GLADYS flounces out to the back room.

DOLLY: Nan?

NAN DEAR: [to herself] Tree? [To DOLLY] You mean the biyala? Spirit tree, branches hanging low over the river?

DOLLY: Like this.

NAN looks over DOLLY's shoulder to see the diagram she is making.

I need to list all our family members ... our parents and their parents and so on ...

NAN picks up a pencil and begins to write over DOLLY's shoulder.

... but not cousins.

NAN stops writing.

NAN DEAR: And why not cousins? What kind of a fool thing ...? You need to know who your cousins are. So you don't marry 'em.

GLADYS returns.

GLADYS: Queen Victoria married her cousin – 'Prince Albert of Saxe-Coburg'.

NAN DEAR: Well, we don't.

DOLLY: [baiting her] And Mum told me that 'our lovely young monarch' married her Greek/German cousin, Prince Philip –

GLADYS: My glory, it was a beautiful wedding –

NAN DEAR: Hmmp. No good'll come of it.

6.1

Check for understanding

1 Use a dictionary or search online to find the meanings of these Aboriginal English and Australian colloquialisms (informal words).

a humpy: __________

b hullabaloo: __________

c squiz: __________

2 In First Nations communities, extended kinship networks work to understand who is responsible for whom as well as maintaining genetic health. Identify a section from the scene that illustrates the subversion of respect and reverence for the Royal Family.

____

____

3 Explain Nan's and Gladys' different **attitudes** towards the Queen's visit.

a Nan: __________

b Gladys: __________

4 What does the stage direction that Gladys listens to the radio 'in rapt silence' communicate about her attitude?

____

attitudes Particular ways of thinking and feeling towards people or things

5 What stage direction could you add to indicate the tone of voice for Nan's line 'One loyal subject in the family is enough'? Explain your choice.

6 What does 'flounce' mean? What does it reveal about Gladys' emotional state as she leaves the room?

7 Explain Nan's reaction to Dolly's homework as revealed through the stage directions.

8 Notions of kinship (family connections) are significant within First Nations cultures. What does Dolly's family tree homework task suggest about the ignorance or insensitivity of the education system at the time?

9 How does the Queen's speech in the opening lines of the scene introduce the overall issue that Harrison is exploring?

Dialogue

Dialogue in a play is like the heart of the performance, driving the story forward and bringing characters to life. It serves several important functions.

- It reveals characterisation: how a character speaks and interacts with others reveals their personality, **values** and motivations.
- It develops relationships: the interactions and exchanges of dialogue between characters.

values Ideas and beliefs specific to individuals and groups

- It advances the plot: the information communicated and conflict developed through dialogue move the story along, as well as building tension and drama.
- It establishes setting and context: clues about the play's setting, time period and cultural **context** are revealed by characters as they speak.
- It conveys themes and **perspectives**: themes are revealed through the topics of conversations, as well as characters' various perspectives on those topics.

Power dynamics are also revealed through dialogue. When studying a play, consider who dominates the conversation and who stays silent. Note whether any characters are cut off or spoken over by others. An ellipsis (…) is used to indicate dialogue trailing off, while a dash (–) can indicate that the speaker has been interrupted or cut off.

Pauses and short silences known as 'beats' can also be important in shaping **audiences**' interpretation of dialogue, allowing them time to contemplate what has just been said.

context An environment or situation (social, cultural or historical) in which a text is responded to or created. Or wording surrounding an unfamiliar word, which a reader or listener uses to understand its meaning
perspective A lens through which the author perceives the world and creates a text, or the lens through which the reader or viewer perceives the world and understands a text
audience An intended or assumed group of readers, listeners or viewers that a writer, designer, filmmaker or speaker is addressing

SCENE ONE (B)

The radio is heard featuring a description of the Queen's 1954 Royal Tour of Australia.

ANNOUNCER: [voice-over] In every town it was something different. In Shepparton, it was babies. My word, babies everywhere! All washed and dressed and fit to meet the band. No wonder the Duke called out, 'Where's Father?'

GLADYS, holding a very wilted bunch of flowers, comes inside the humpy and plonks down in the only chair. She kicks off her shoes. DOLLY watches her. NAN is cooking.

GLADYS: Oh, my feet! Remind me never to borrow Aunty's shoes again.

NAN DEAR: What about the taxi?

GLADYS: Didn't show, did it? So I walked up to the causeway –

NAN DEAR: That's not far.

GLADYS: Then all the way to Shepp.

NAN DEAR: To Shepp? Why?

GLADYS: On account of the hessian.

NAN DEAR: What hessian?

GLADYS: The hessian they lined the road with. The hessian that I couldn't get through and couldn't even peek over.

DOLLY: What they do that for?

GLADYS: Stop the likes of her seeing our humpies.

NAN DEAR: Dolly, bring the wood in.

DOLLY sighs and exits.

GLADYS: If they'd given us better houses ... But hessian! Like a band-aid over a sore –

NAN DEAR: What are they going to do with all that hessian?

GLADYS: Oh, Mum, doesn't it bother you?

NAN DEAR: What good is it if I get het up? My job is to get food on the table –

GLADYS: But decent housing, Mum –

NAN DEAR: Gladys, get off your high horse. Least here we do things our way – no one breathin' down our necks. Not like those last days at Cummeragunja. [Beat.] Anyway, it's Papa Dear's mission to make things better for the Aboriginal people. [Beat.] Papa Dear had a meetin' with her, you know.

GLADYS: Our head of state? He had a meeting? With our queen?

NAN DEAR: She's not my queen. But yes, that's how important –

GLADYS: – he is.

NAN DEAR: – she is – getting a meeting with the busiest Aboriginal around!

GLADYS: Why didn't you tell me?

NAN DEAR: I just did. He popped in to see us. But you were out gallivanting.

GLADYS: I missed him ...? Did he say what she was like?

NAN DEAR: For goodness' sake!

DOLLY returns and is listening with interest.

GLADYS: And I was just hoping for a glimpse.

DOLLY: Did you get one?

GLADYS: No ...

NAN DEAR: Gawd, daught, where do you get these highfalutin ideas from?

GLADYS: Well, it's either from you, or it's from Papa Dear, and somehow I don't think it's from –

NAN DEAR: Don't just sit there, girl. Stoke the fire.

DOLLY: Yes, Nan.

GLADYS: Yes, Mum.

The radio fades up again.

ANNOUNCER: [voice-over] And just to remind the royal couple that they were in Australia, we showed them how to throw a boomerang ... It really does come back ...

The lights go down.

6.2

Check for understanding

1 Circle the words that best describe how Gladys feels as she returns home from trying to see the Queen. You can choose more than one.

frustrated	pleased	satisfied	disappointed	optimistic
defeated	outraged	patriotic	elated	bitter

2 Explain how the following parts of Gladys' dialogue help to reveal her mood:

a the rhetorical question 'Didn't show, did it?'

____

b the repetition of 'hessian'

____

c the exclamation 'Oh, Mum, doesn't it bother you?'

____

3 Why have the roads around the Flats been lined with hessian? Support your answer with evidence from the text.

____

____

4 Note the use of an ellipsis after Gladys says 'If they'd given us better houses …' What do you think the unfinished thought might be?

____

____

5 What do you think Gladys means when she says the hessian screens are like 'a band-aid over a sore'? What does this suggest about government policies of the time and their support for First Nations communities?

____

____

____

6 Re-read the following lines.

> NAN DEAR: What good is it if I get het up? My job is to get food on the table –
>
> GLADYS: But decent housing, Mum –

a What does the dash at the end of each line indicate?

b What does this exchange reveal about Nan's and Gladys' different priorities?

7 Why do you think there is a beat after 'those last days at Cummeragunja'?

8 How does Nan's reference to Cummeragunja help the audience understand her apparent lack of interest in the issue of decent housing?

9 Re-read the part of the exchange between Nan and Gladys in which Nan reveals that Papa Dear met with the Queen. Explain how their dialogue reveals their different perspectives regarding Papa Dear's importance as a leader in contrast to the Queen's.

10 What does the radio announcer's comment at the end of this scene reveal about Australia's sometimes paradoxical (seemingly contradictory) treatment of First Nations peoples and cultures? Explain your answer using evidence from this extract.

Dramatic irony

Dramatic irony is a clever literary technique commonly used in plays. It happens when the audience knows something important that the characters don't know. This creates suspense and sometimes humour the audience watches the characters make decisions without this significant knowledge and eagerly waits to see how it all unfolds.

In *Rainbow's End*, the prologue reveals that the family's humpy has been devastated by floodwaters. But when Scene One (A) begins, the flood is yet to happen.

PROLOGUE: AFTERMATH

The song 'Que sera, sera' is heard:

Que sera, sera

Whatever will be, will be,

The future's not ours to see

Que sera, sera.

It's late spring, late afternoon and gloomy outside. Inside their humpy NAN DEAR and GLADYS are rebuilding after a flood has devastated their home. Everything below three feet is sodden and mud-splattered. GLADYS mops, wrings out and removes things that are destroyed. NAN finishes hanging a piece of hessian to replace a ruined piece that lined the interior walls. Now she covers the hessian with pages from a magazine.

NAN DEAR: [pointing to some magazines] Pass those.

GLADYS: They're Dolly's.

NAN DEAR: They're dry.

GLADYS hands them over. NAN rips the pages, slowly and deliberately, pastes them with homemade glue and sticks them, upside down, onto the hessian. After a time DOLLY arrives home from school and surveys the scene critically. She toes the old, ruined lino. She sighs, resigned, until she spots her magazines. She goes to protest but sighs again, resigned. GLADYS fakes cheerfulness.

GLADYS: It'll be all right.

DOLLY: You always say that.

NAN and GLADYS take a quick look at each other. NAN gestures for DOLLY to come over. She does and NAN gives her granddaughter a hug.

The lights go down.

6.3 Reflecting and discussing

Discuss the following questions in pairs, in small groups or with the whole class as directed by your teacher.

1 How would the prologue of *Rainbow's End* function to create dramatic irony as the audience then watches Scene One (A) and (B)?

2 What does the prologue reveal about the strength and resilience of the Dear family?

3 How does the use of the song 'Que Sera, Sera' ('Whatever will be, will be') reinforce both the dramatic irony and the play's theme of resilience?

4 Nan's dialogue in Scene One (B) reveals that Papa Dear is an 'important' figure in improving conditions for First Nations people. Why do you think Harrison chooses instead to focus on the women of this family?

6.4 Get creative

A monologue is a powerful form of drama in which a single character speaks aloud for an extended period of time, presenting their thoughts, emotions or experiences to an audience. It allows for an intimate glimpse into the character's mind and can be a compelling way to convey a story, share a perspective or explore complex themes in a theatrical setting. A monologue can be a standalone piece of theatre or incorporated into a longer play.

Follow the steps to compose and deliver a monologue.

1 Select a current social issue that you feel passionate about or one that you believe deserves attention. It could be related to climate change, rural disadvantage, gender equality, social media impact, or any other relevant topic that affects our society today.

2 Do thorough research to understand the various perspectives on your chosen social issue. Gather statistics, personal stories and credible sources to support your understanding of its complexities.

3 Create a character to deliver the monologue. This character should be deeply connected to the social issue you have chosen. Consider their background, beliefs and values, as well as their experiences of the issue, to make them authentic and easy to relate to.

4 Determine the **purpose** of your monologue. Are you trying to raise awareness, evoke empathy or encourage action? Knowing your purpose will shape the **tone** and content of your character's monologue.

5 Draft your monologue. It should tell a compelling story or share a personal experience related to the social issue. Use vivid language, descriptive details and emotional appeals to engage the audience and draw them into the character's world.

6 Add stage directions, incorporating instructions about movement, gesture, facial expressions, tone or even costume and props that might enhance the impact of your monologue.

7 Proofread and **edit** your monologue, ensuring that each line is crafted for maximum impact. Try reading it aloud a couple of times to be certain that it sounds authentic for your character.

8 Rehearse your monologue in front of a mirror, experimenting with your vocal delivery (pace, volume, intonation etc.) until you feel it reflects your character and fulfils your intended purpose. Try to learn it off by heart. You might even record a rehearsal and play it back to yourself to improve your performance.

9 Seek feedback by performing the monologue for a trusted peer or family member.

10 Wow your classmates with your performance! Host a monologue evening or a lunchtime performance, or just collaborate in the classroom, listening to each other's monologues and engaging in post-performance discussions of the issues explored. You could even invite some teachers or drama students to act as a panel to review your performances.

If you find the thought of being solo on stage too challenging, you could write a script involving two characters, using the **conventions** you have explored in *Rainbow's End*, and perform it with a friend.

purpose An intended or assumed reason for a type of text
tone The mood created by the language features used by an author and the way the text makes the reader feel
edit To prepare, alter, adapt or refine with attention to grammar, spelling, punctuation and vocabulary
convention An accepted practice that has developed over time and is generally used and understood (e.g. use of punctuation)

UNIT 7

Finding your voice

Every day, people speak up about what matters to them. Whether they share an experience, draw attention to an injustice or persuade others to help make the world a better place, speeches and presentations can be a powerful force for change. At the same time, many people find the thought of speaking to an audience a daunting prospect. So how can you become a better speaker? How can you make sure that your voice stands out in the crowd?

In this unit, you will learn:

- about the features of spoken texts
- how language is used to position listeners
- how to craft your own persuasive speech.

Curriculum content

Australian Curriculum content description	Content code
Understand how language can have inclusive and exclusive social effects, and can empower or disempower people.	AC9E10LA01
Analyse how meaning and style are achieved through syntax.	AC9E10LA06
Listen to spoken texts and explain the purposes and effects of text structures and language features, and use interaction skills to discuss and present an opinion about these texts.	AC9E10LY02
Plan, create, rehearse and deliver spoken and multimodal presentations by experimenting with rhetorical devices, and the organisation and development of ideas, to engage audiences for different purposes in ways that may be imaginative, reflective, informative, persuasive, analytical and/or critical.	AC9E10LY07

TED Talks

TED Talks are short, powerful presentations delivered by speakers from various fields and backgrounds. They are hosted by an American-Canadian non-profit media organisation whose slogan is 'Ideas worth spreading'. TED stands for 'Technology, Entertainment, Design', which were the original focus areas when the talks began in 1984. However, TED Talks have since expanded to cover an even wider range of topics, including science, art, business, education and culture. Communities all over the world organise TED-style events. The speeches given at these events are called TEDx Talks.

TED Talks aim to inspire and stimulate thoughtful conversations, providing a platform for experts, innovators and leaders to share their knowledge and experiences with **audiences**.

audience An intended or assumed group of readers, listeners or viewers that a writer, designer, filmmaker or speaker is addressing

7.1 Reflecting and discussing

Discuss the following questions in pairs, in small groups or with the whole class as directed by your teacher.

1 Have you listened to a TED Talk or watched one online? What was it about? Did you find it interesting? Why or why not?

2 Search the internet to watch a speech by one of these inspirational people: Malala Yousafzai, Jessica Watson, Jack Manning Bancroft, Greta Thunberg or Omar Musa. Did you find the speech inspirational or engaging? Why or why not?

In a presentation delivered at a TEDx event in Melbourne in 2015, Thomas King, Victorian Young Australian of the Year 2015, talked about the issue of supporting young people to plan for a future in a world that will be quite different from the world today. Scan the QR code to watch his TEDx Talk.

Read the beginning of King's speech below.

It's time we had the talk. When two people love each other very ... No, I'm kidding. Not that talk, although this one might be just as uncomfortable. Let me explain.

By 2035, I will be 39. Disruptive businesses like Uber and Airbnb will have revolutionised entire markets with driverless cars and innovative renting services. Two-thirds of our world will live in cities. Social enterprises that help the community and planet will prevail over traditional business and charity models and our entire society will be cashless, with a shift to electronic money. But here's the thing. From the moment I was born, I had a cultural narrative set out in front of me that I'm expected to follow, which is based on the twentieth century. Go to school, learn from a set curriculum, achieve good grades, complete a degree, get a HECS debt, work nine to five, climb the ladder, earn more money, buy more things, get a mortgage, reproduce, and then place the same expectations on my children.

When I look at this narrative, I can't help but wonder, isn't it based on the assumption that the world of tomorrow is going to resemble the world of today? Our economy, workforce and industries are changing rapidly due to automation, artificial intelligence, digital disruption, but also a shift in mindset, because people don't want to work just any job; we want to do something meaningful with our lives.

I'm not a futurist, so I don't know for sure what our world will look like in 20 years, but what I can guarantee you is that it won't look anything like it does today. So why on earth are we raising the next generation to live the same lives as previous generations? To me, it makes no logical sense.

Now, as a young person standing up here today questioning this path, I'm not rejecting earlier generations; I'm not placing blame; I'm not giving up. I'm simply saying we need to have the talk, and it's an uncomfortable one, but it's one that's everybody's responsibility – my generation included.

7.2 Check for understanding

1 What does King mean by the following **phrases**?

a disruptive businesses: ____________________

b social enterprises: ____________________

c cultural narrative: ____________________

d climb the ladder: ____________________

e shift in mindset: ____________________

2 Why does King believe the 'world of tomorrow' is going to be radically different from today's world?

3 What is the problem or issue identified by King about how 'the next generation' is being raised?

4 King repeats the idea that discussing the need for a new and innovative way of preparing young people for the future might be an 'uncomfortable' talk. Why do you think it might be uncomfortable for many of the adults in the audience?

phrase A group of words often beginning with a preposition but without a subject and verb combination (e.g. 'on the river'; 'with brown eyes')

Spoken language features

When giving a speech or presentation, speakers manipulate their vocal control in various ways, to enhance their communication and convey their attitudes and emotions while ensuring that the audience comprehends the message they want to deliver.

Some of the main spoken **language features** and their effects are:

- pace: the speed or rate of speaking, which can be adjusted to create emphasis or convey a sense of urgency or calm
- rhythm: the fluency and modulation (variation) when speaking, which can be manipulated to engage listeners, create emphasis or support the structure of a speech
- intonation: variations in pitch (the perceived highness or lowness of a voice), which adds nuance to language, indicating questions or statements and communicating the speaker's attitude
- volume: the loudness or softness of a voice, which not only contributes to the projection of a speaker's voice but is also used to build intensity or create mood

language features Features that support meaning e.g. clause- and word-level grammar, vocabulary, figurative language, punctuation, images. Choices vary for the purpose, subject matter, audience and mode or medium

- pause: brief periods of silence, which can add emphasis to what has just been said, provide time for reflection or comprehension, create suspense or simply indicate a new point of discussion
- tone: the emotional quality of the voice, which reflects the speaker's attitude, mood or intention
- clarity: the clear articulation and enunciation (clear pronunciation) of words and sounds, which ensure that the speaker is understood by the listener.

These are aided by the speaker's eye contact, body language, gesture and movement about the stage.

7.3 Check for understanding

Watch the first two and a half minutes of Thomas King's TEDx Talk and then answer the questions below.

1 How would you describe the overall tone used by King in this section of his speech? Circle the words below that fit best.

aggressive	critical	gentle	matter-of-fact
optimistic	conversational	bored	unconcerned
friendly	direct		

2 Listen carefully to the first sentence of the speech.

a Underline the three words in the following sentence that King emphasises as he speaks: 'It's time we had the talk.'

b How does this use of emphasis draw attention to what King thinks is important?

____

____

3 Watch and listen carefully when King lists the various steps in the 'cultural narrative' that he has been expected to follow (1:02–1:18).

a What does he do with his hands? ______________________________

b What happens to the pace of his speech? ______________________________

c What happens to his intonation? Does it rise or fall? ______________________________

d How do these choices enhance the point he is making? ______________________________

____

____

4 When King says, 'When I look at this narrative, I can't help but wonder, isn't it based on the assumption that the world of tomorrow is going to resemble the world of today?' (1:19–1:28), he uses a rising inflection. What does this indicate? Tick the best answer below.

a He is asking a question. ☐

b He finds the idea difficult to believe. ☐

c He is trying to present this challenging idea gently. ☐

d All of the above. ☐

5 Within the sentence transcribed in question 4, King pauses briefly after 'assumption', 'tomorrow' and 'today'. Why do you think he does this?

____

____

6 Find an example of each of the following two gestures and explain why King uses it.

a ticking things off on his fingers

____

____

b spreading his hands wide

____

____

7 Use the internet to help you create a list of ten different words that might describe the tone of a speech. Try to include a balance of positive and negative terms. An example of each is provided.

Positive	Negative
admiring	pessimistic

Engaging the audience

It is important for speakers to engage their audience, which means to capture and maintain their listeners' interest in what they are saying. Audiences won't stay tuned in for very long if they feel that a speaker is boring, clumsy or ill-prepared. Also, it is important to remember that audiences are *listening* to a speech. They don't have the benefit of going back and re-reading a part they found unclear or difficult like they can with a book.

Here are some ways in which effective speakers engage their audiences.

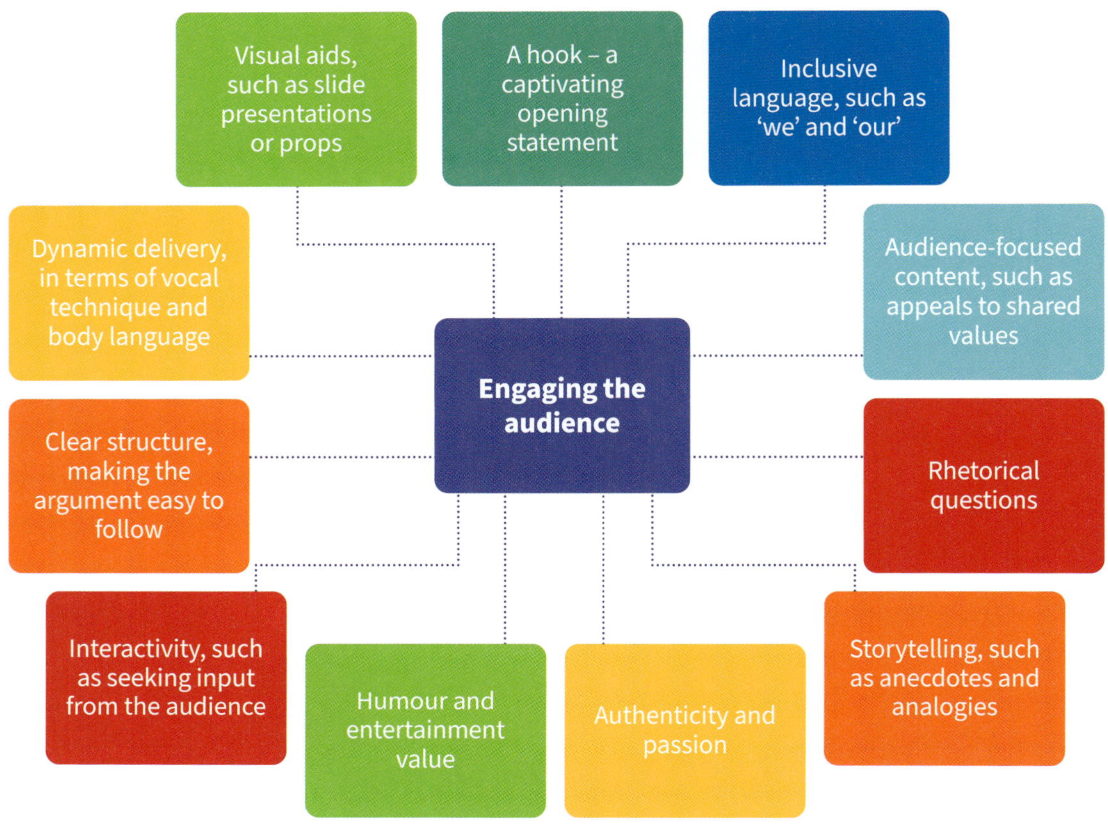

7.4 Check for understanding

1 Think of those teachers or other speakers whom you find most engaging. What techniques do they use that capture and hold your attention?

2 Which of the techniques in the diagram does Thomas King use to engage his audience? Identify four techniques and provide an example of each one from his TEDx Talk.

____

____

____

____

3 How does King's use of personal anecdotes (stories about his own experience) suggest his authenticity in speaking on this topic?

____

____

Persuasive structures

You are probably familiar with the typical linear argument structure, in which a contention (a thesis or viewpoint) is stated and then followed by a series of three or four supporting points of argument. However, there are other ways in which an argument can be structured effectively, depending on the topic.

7.5

Check for understanding

Draw lines to match each type of persuasive structure with its definition in the table below. One has been done for you.

linear	Identify a problem or issue, outline its causes and several effects, then offer a proposed action to solve it.
problem–solution	Offer a proposal, outline the advantages and disadvantages, then advise which side is preferable.
cause–effect–proposal	State a contention followed by several supporting points of argument in a sequential order.
need–plan–benefits	Outline the issue, examine various alternatives while highlighting their similarities and differences, then advise which choice is preferable.
pros–cons–advice	Convince the audience they have a need of some kind, offer a plan to meet that need, and outline the resulting benefits.
comparison/contrast	Outline both sides of an argument, then present a new proposition that incorporates elements of both sides.
thesis–antithesis–synthesis	Identify a problem, then offer solutions.

In his TEDx Talk, Thomas King uses the 'cause–effect–proposal' structure:

» Problem:

The current cultural narrative (the expectations of what life should look like) does not help to prepare future generations for a vastly different world.

» Causes:

1 Changes in context mean the current world is already very different from the world of the twentieth century, and the future world can only be more different.

2 Changes in young people's sense of purpose mean they now want a more meaningful and less materialistic life.

» Effects:

1 Young people fail to see the relevance of the current education system.

2 Materialism does not make people feel fulfilled.

» Proposal:

We need a new cultural narrative that reflects the skills and qualities that future generations will need.

7.6

Check for understanding

Listen to the rest of King's TEDx Talk.

1 Identify evidence from King's presentation that supports each stage listed in the 'cause–effect–proposal' structure above.

a Problem: ________________________

b Cause 1: ________________________

c Cause 2: ________________________

d Effect 1: ________________________

e Effect 2: ________________________

f Proposal: ________________________

2 Why do you think King includes the example of his own impressive achievements, which were attained outside his 'thankfully' flexible school?

3 Identify other evidence that King uses to support the following arguments:

a the future world will be very different

___

b young people want a more purposeful life

___

4 King includes a counter-argument – an acknowledgement of a point in opposition to his own. He notes that not all young people's motivations are the same.

a What are some young people motivated by, according to King?

___

b Why do you think he includes this point even though it might detract from his own argument that young people want to make a difference in the world?

___

___

___

Persuasive techniques

Writers of persuasive speeches use a variety of techniques to engage with and have an impact on their audience. These techniques are sometimes grouped in terms of their overall persuasive or rhetorical functions, using a range of Greek terms that have come down through history from the Ancient Greek philosopher, Aristotle.

jargon Technical words specific to a certain group, such as medical or legal jargon

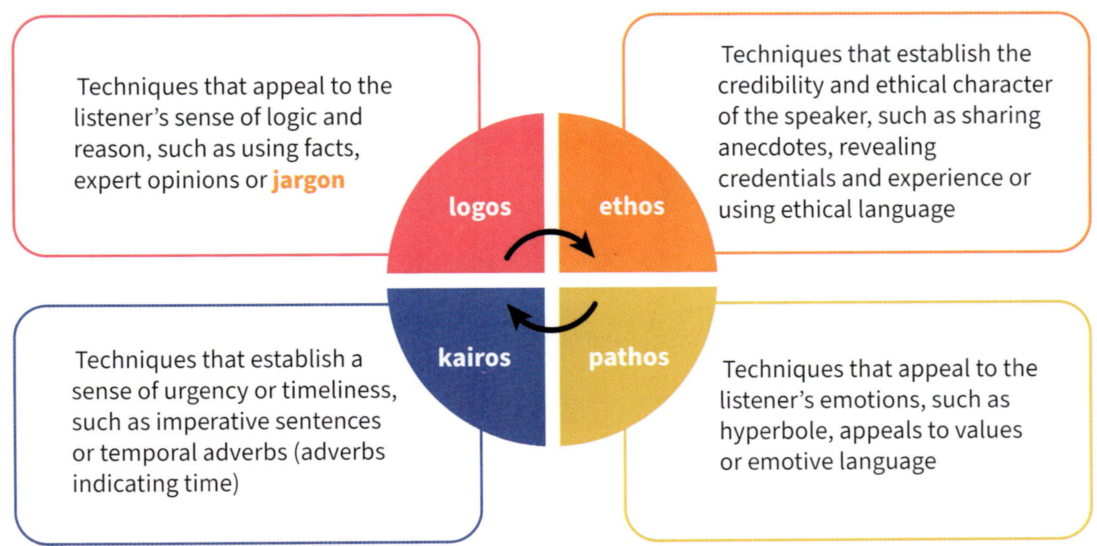

7.7

Check for understanding

1 Write the following terms in the correct spaces below to match each persuasive technique with its explanation.

value appeal	rhetorical question	social proof
facts and statistics	repetition	emotive language
anecdotes	figurative language	inclusive language
expert opinions	call to action	hyperbole
listing		

a using words and phrases that evoke strong emotions in the audience:

____

b providing objective information, data or numbers to support an argument:

____

c asking a question that is not meant to be answered but aims to make the audience think: ______________________________

d referring to statements from authoritative or knowledgeable people to add credibility to an argument: ______________________________

e using **metaphors**, **similes** or other figures of speech to create vivid **imagery**:

____

f appealing to the audience's **values**, such as nationalism or the family, to persuade them by aligning with what they consider important:

____

g encouraging the audience to take a specific action, make a decision or change their behaviour: ______________________________

h sharing personal stories or examples to illustrate a point, engage the audience and make the message easier to relate to: ______________________________

metaphor A type of figurative language used to describe a person or object through an implicit comparison to something with similar characteristics
simile A device comparing 2 things that are not alike. Similes use 'like', 'as' or 'than' to make the comparison (e.g. The cake was as light as air)
imagery Visually descriptive or figurative language to represent things including objects, actions and ideas in ways that appeal to the senses of the reader or viewer
values Ideas and beliefs specific to individuals and groups

i repeating words, phrases or ideas to reinforce a message: ________________

j using testimonials, endorsements or examples of other people to show that a particular idea is accepted or valued by a larger group: ________________

k using words and phrases that include and address the audience directly, making them feel involved and part of the message: ________________

l using exaggerated statements or claims for emphasis or dramatic effect to make a point or persuade the audience: ________________

m including a series of three or more ideas, qualities or outcomes in order to emphasise the scale of the topic: ________________

2 Read this short extract from King's TEDx Talk.

> If knowledge is power, how will we use this incredible power we now possess? My generation is set on doing something, a purpose. Having access to an abundance of knowledge is exciting, but it also exposes the shadows in our society: social inequality, economic disparity, conflict, poverty, animal abuse, environmental exploitation, and a population who, let's be honest, are mostly in debt, dispassionate about their work, and in a state of physical and mental dis-ease. I don't need to spout the figures; we all know these are serious problems. You don't need to be the Dalai Lama to realise you can't find purpose in material wealth.

Identify the persuasive technique used by King in each of the following quotes:

a 'how will we use this incredible power we now possess?' ________________

b 'the shadows in our society' ________________

c 'social inequality, economic disparity, conflict, poverty ...' ________________

d 'a population who ... are mostly in debt, dispassionate about their work, and in a state of physical and mental disease' ________________

e 'we all know these are serious problems' ________________

f 'You don't need to be the Dalai Lama to realise you can't find purpose in material wealth.' ________________

3 Overall, how persuasive did you find King's argument? Did he convince you that a 'new cultural narrative' is needed for today's young people? Explain your answer.

____

____

____

____

Analysing sentences

When writing an effective speech, it is important to have a thorough grasp of syntax – the arrangement of words and phrases to create well-formed sentences. More than simply aiming for variety, good writers construct sentences to improve clarity and enhance the effects they generate.

Sentences can be described in terms of structure.

» A *simple sentence* consists of a single independent clause, which contains a subject and a verb and expresses a complete thought. For example: 'Erin ran to catch the bus.'

» A *compound sentence* consists of two or more independent clauses that are connected by a coordinating conjunction (such as 'and', 'but' or 'or') or a semicolon. For example: 'Paul studied hard for the exam, and he passed with flying colours.'

» A *complex sentence* consists of an independent clause and at least one dependent clause. The dependent clause relies on the independent clause to form a complete thought. For example: 'Although she was tired, Amber decided to go to the party.'

» A *compound-complex sentence* contains two or more independent clauses and at least one dependent clause. For example: 'Despite the fact it was raining, I decided to go for a walk, and I took my umbrella in case it got heavier.'

Sentences can also be described in terms of type.

» A *declarative sentence* makes a statement or expresses a fact, opinion or idea, such as 'The sun is shining brightly today.'

» An *interrogative sentence* asks a direct question, such as 'What time is the meeting?'

» An *imperative sentence* gives a command, instruction or request, such as 'Please close the door quietly.'

» An *exclamatory sentence* expresses strong emotion, surprise or excitement, such as 'What a beautiful dog!'

Some techniques that writers use to construct persuasive sentences include:

- tricolon: a group of three parallel words, phrases, clauses or sentences. For example: 'These holidays, I'm going to relax, socialise with friends and catch up on my reading.'
- anaphora: the repetition of a word or phrase at the beginning of successive phrases, clauses or sentences. For example: 'We shall fight on the beaches, we shall fight on the landing grounds, we shall fight in the fields and in the streets …'
- parallelism: the use of similar grammatical structures to communicate various ideas, suggesting symmetry or comparison. For example: 'I know social media can be a problem. Everybody knows social media can be a problem.'
- antithesis: the juxtaposition of contrasting ideas, words or phrases to create a sense of opposition or comparison. For example: 'It was the best of times, it was the worst of times …'
- polysyndeton: when conjunctions (such as 'and', 'or' and 'but') are deliberately and repeatedly used in close succession to create a sense of emphasis or rhythm or to suggest a feeling of abundance. For example: 'I ate pizza and pasta and salad and bread – and then dessert.'
- asyndeton: when conjunctions are intentionally omitted between words, phrases or clauses, resulting in a faster pace and a more concise expression. For example: 'I came, I saw, I conquered.'

Abstraction and nominalisation

Abstraction and nominalisation are two other ways in which writers can manipulate language to enhance communication.

- 'Abstraction' is the expression of broad concepts rather than specific, tangible objects or actions. It can be used to convey complex ideas concisely. For example, we might discuss 'pollution' rather than trying to list all the specific types of pollution, such as smog, carbon emissions, landfill toxicity, industrial run-off, pesticide residue and so on.
- 'Nominalisation' is the transformation of verbs or other parts of speech into nouns. It is commonly used to create more formal or academic language, as well as to emphasise concepts, ideas or states rather than specific actions or individuals. For example, 'discussion' is a nominalisation of the verb 'to discuss'.

7.8 Check for understanding

1 In his TEDx Talk, Thomas King uses a variety of sentence structures. Read the extract, and then read the list of sentence types labelled a–e below. Match each type of sentence to a sentence in the extract by writing the label letter next to the corresponding extract sentence. Some sentences have more than one descriptor.

Isn't it remarkable that the context we now live in allows us to pursue our purpose and create choose-your-own-adventure lives rather than 'thanks for 31 years of service, here's an engraved pen'? ________________

So, let's stop trying to push our dated expectations onto young people. ________________

We need to evolve. ________________

So, can't we instead foster and encourage innovation and creativity, entrepreneurialism, financial literacy, and critical thinking, rather than stuffing information in young people's heads and saying, 'Now follow this path'? ________________

Instead of asking me what job I wanted to go into, I wanted my parents and teachers and aunts and neighbours to ask what I'm passionate about, what I desire, what kind of society I want to live in, and how I could create a legacy to help make that place a reality. ________________

a A very short, simple sentence that draws attention to a specific point.

b An example of listing that emphasises a range of desirable qualities.

c An interrogative sentence that gets the audience thinking.

d An example of anaphora that draws attention to three points.

e An imperative sentence that instructs the audience.

2 Identify an example of each of the following in the extract:

a abstraction: ________________________________

b nominalisation: ________________________________

3 Would you agree that King's choice of language creates a credible (believable) and convincing voice? Why or why not? Discuss with a partner.

4 Read the closing paragraph of King's TEDx Talk.

> Because it's the role of each generation to forge a new path, but that progress can happen so much quicker with the support of other generations. So now that we've had the talk, I have a proposition for you: let's work together to take advantage of today's context, design a new purposeful narrative, and fulfil our obligation of overcoming humanity's current challenges. Because then we can do the same with the next generation.

Explain the persuasive techniques that King uses to present his closing proposal to the audience.

____

____

____

____

____

5 Do you think that King's TEDx Talk is an example of an effective speech? Justify your response.

____

____

____

____

____

7.9 Get creative

Create a TEDx Talk of your own to share your **perspective** on an issue or topic of importance to you. Follow the steps to create your TEDx Talk.

1 Decide on your topic. What are you passionate about? What insights do you have that you might share with others? Try to draw on something from your own experience. For example, you might want to speak about dwindling water resources and the impact of this on your farming community, or the implications of artificial intelligence for your education.

2 Consider your audience. Who are you aiming this speech at? What do you know about their backgrounds and values? Why you think this audience needs to hear this speech? What **style** of argument is likely to appeal to them?

3 Focus on your purpose. What do you want your audience to understand, feel or do as a result of your speech? Use this purpose to develop your contention – the argument you want to make.

4 Undertake some research. In order for your argument to be credible, it needs to have some genuine facts behind it. However, balance this out with personal stories – either yours or other people's. This helps to humanise the issue.

5 Develop a list of supporting arguments. Based on your experience and research, identify three or four points that you can make to support your contention. Make sure you have evidence to support each point.

6 Determine the appropriate structure for your speech, based on your topic, such as a problem–solution or comparison structure. You will need an engaging opening (a hook), as well as a call to action (if necessary) to conclude your speech.

7 Draft your TEDx Talk. Use a variety of persuasive techniques that target your specific audience, but remember to be authentic, too. Your speech will be more effective if your passion and personality shine through. Aim for a range of ethos, pathos and logos strategies, and include kairos if appropriate:

   a ethos: why should people listen to you?

   b pathos: what emotions are you trying to evoke in the audience?

   c logos: how will you convince them that your argument makes sense?

   d kairos: why is now the time to act?

8 Rehearse. Practise your speech several times, until you become familiar with it. Experiment with your vocal techniques to ensure that your speaking voice is convincing and impactful. You might even video yourself and watch your performance to improve your delivery, or seek feedback from a peer or parent.

9 Deliver your TEDx Talk. Organise a mini-TEDx event with others in your class, at which you share your TEDx Talks and admire the wealth of knowledge and passion in your classroom!

perspective A lens through which the author perceives the world and creates a text, or the lens through which the reader or viewer perceives the world and understands a text
style The distinctive language features, text structures and/or subject matter in a text which may shape meaning, be enjoyed for its aesthetic qualities or distinguish the work of an author, period etc.

UNIT 8

Multimodal evolution

Technology evolves constantly, providing creators of texts with amazing opportunities to develop new and interesting ways of storytelling. Graphic novels, in both print and digital media, provide an excellent illustration of how a genre can develop in response to new technologies. Working with pen and paper, creators of traditional graphic novels use a range of techniques to suggest movement and sound in their illustrations. The digital graphic novel, however, is able to enhance the traditional modes of image and text with actual sound, motion and even interactivity, inviting readers to participate in the making of the story. We can only wonder what exciting adventures technology will take us on in the future!

In this unit, you will learn:

- about the conventions of graphic novels
- how technology has generated new forms of storytelling
- about the concept of aesthetics.

Note to teacher: The pages included in this unit are from the graphic novel *Illegal* and may be difficult to read. For successful completion of this unit, it is suggested that the graphic novel be purchased and displayed in class.

Curriculum content

Australian Curriculum content description	Content code
Analyse text structures and language features and evaluate their effectiveness in achieving their purpose.	AC9E10LA03
Evaluate the features of still and moving images, and the effects of those choices on representations.	AC9E10LA07
Analyse how the aesthetic qualities associated with text structures, language features, literary devices and visual features, and the context in which these texts are experienced, influence audience response.	AC9E10LE03
Analyse and evaluate the aesthetic qualities of texts.	AC9E10LE07
Analyse and evaluate how language features are used to implicitly or explicitly represent values, beliefs and attitudes.	AC9E10LY03

The graphic novel

The graphic novel is a captivating form of storytelling that combines the art of illustration with the power of the written word. The term 'graphic novel' was first coined in 1964 to describe comics collected into albums. It became popular after Will Eisner's *A Contract with God* was published in 1978. The earliest example, however, is thought to be an 1837 publication by Swiss cartoonist Rodolphe Töpffer, *The Adventures of Mr Obadiah Oldbuck*.

Covering a wide range of genres, such as fantasy, science fiction and memoir, graphic novels have become an incredibly popular form of narrative.

Illegal, by Eoin Colfer and Andrew Donkin and illustrated by Giovanni Rigano, tells the tale of Ebo, a 12-year-old boy from Africa, who manages to travel on a small boat headed for Italy after escaping from people traffickers. Based on real-life accounts of asylum seekers, this is a powerful and tragic story of the challenges faced by those who seek a better life away from their homelands.

Read the opening of chapter 1 below.

8.1

Check for understanding

1 Use an atlas or online map to locate Ghana, Niger, Algeria, Libya and Italy to gain a sense of the scale of Ebo's journey.

2 This image is set in the Mediterranean Sea, between Libya and Italy, where Ebo is on a small rubber dinghy with 13 other passengers. Why do you think the composers have used a double-page spread for this image?

____

____

3 The rubber dinghy is small and located in the lower third of the image. How does this make the boat and its passengers seem vulnerable?

____

____

4 What is symbolised by the presence of the wake trailing behind the boat in contrast to the unbroken expanse of water ahead?

____

____

5 What might Ebo mean by the comment 'I think he might be right'?

____

____

6 How has the illustrator created a sense of movement in the water?

____

____

7 Some of the text is in a speech bubble, while the rest is in a series of square boxes. What might be the purpose of this distinction?

____

____

Conventions of graphic novels

The key conventions of graphic novels include:

- *panels:* individual frames or boxes that contain a specific scene or moment. Illustrators play with different sizes and shapes of panels for meaning and effect. For example, a large panel will often be used for important or dramatic scenes.
- *borders:* each panel is usually surrounded by a border. Different borders can suggest different sorts of transitions between scenes.
- *gutters:* spaces between panels, which can be manipulated to create effects such as time passing.
- *speech balloons or bubbles:* dialogue is often presented in balloons, which are typically connected to the character speaking. Different shapes and styles of word balloons may be used to convey different emotions or tones.
- *captions:* these can provide additional narration, such as a character's inner thoughts, or descriptive text.
- *sound effects:* visual representations of sounds are commonly depicted using onomatopoeia or stylised lettering.
- *page layout:* the arrangement of panels and images on a page is an essential aspect of graphic novel storytelling.
- *artistic style:* graphic novels encompass a wide range of artistic styles, from highly realistic to abstract or cartoonish. The visual style chosen by the artist contributes to the overall tone and atmosphere of the story.
- *sequence:* the arrangement and progression of panels and pages in a graphic novel form a sequence of visual events, allowing the story to unfold over time.
- *colours:* specific colours are often used to convey mood, atmosphere or **symbolism**.
- *page-turn:* graphic novels take advantage of the physicality of the medium, utilising page-turns as a storytelling device. Reveals, surprises or changes in **perspective** can be timed to occur at specific moments when the reader turns the page.
- *symbolism and* ***metaphor****:* graphic novels use symbols and visual metaphors to add depth and meaning to the story.

symbolism The use of one object, person or situation to signify or represent another by giving them meanings that are different from their literal sense (e.g. a dove is a symbol of peace)
perspective A lens through which the author perceives the world and creates a text, or the lens through which the reader or viewer perceives the world and understands a text
metaphor A type of figurative language used to describe a person or object through an implicit comparison to something with similar characteristics

Read the next two pages of *Illegal*.

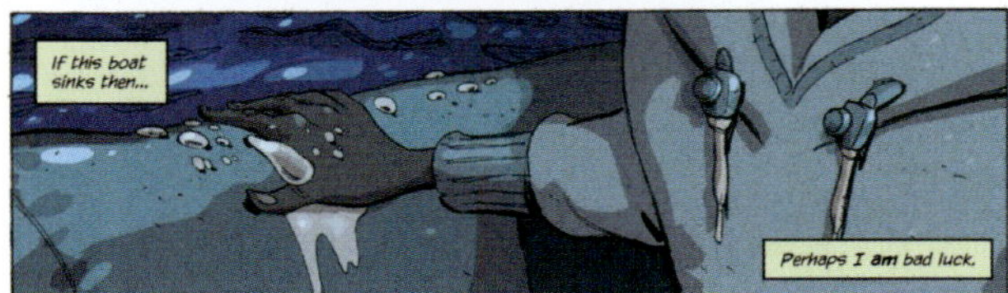

8.2

Check for understanding

1. The five panels on page 4 are all the same size and shape, but they frame the argument between Nuru and Kwame from different perspectives. What effect does this create?

   ____

   ____

2. Describe the expression on Nuru's face in the second panel on page 4.

   ____

   ____

3. The second panel on page 5 features a close-up on Ebo and a single word.

   a. Why is 'STOP!' in capital letters? ______________________

   b. What emotion is shown on Ebo's face? ______________________

c Why have the creators chosen to focus on just Ebo in this moment?

4 Why does Nuru believe it is bad luck to have Ebo on the boat? What does his comment suggest about the risks that asylum seekers are prepared to take?

5 The first panel on page 5 looks different than other panels.

a Why do you think the creators have chosen to use a different colour palette and a less clearly defined border here?

b What does this panel suggest about the perilous conditions that asylum seekers have to endure?

c How is a sense of turbulence or danger created in this panel?

d What is suggested by the larger size of this panel?

Creating movement in still images

Creators of graphic novels use a range of clever tricks to imply a sense of movement within their images, manipulating the sizes and shapes of their panels and the angles from which they depict their **subject matter**, as well as the juxtaposition (placing things side by side) of images in sequential panels.

subject matter The topic or theme under consideration

Read this sequence of four pages from *Illegal*, which contrasts Ebo's journey through the desert to get to Libya with the boat journey to Italy.

8.3

Check for understanding

1 How does the sequence of panels on page 82 create the impression that the group of characters is approaching the reader from a great distance?

2 On page 83, what is implied by the sequence of the second, third and fourth panels?

3 Page 84 shows the impact of a page-turn reveal.

a What effect is created by the double-page spread?

b What does the high angle reveal about the boat?

c How is a sense of movement created around the helicopter's rotor blades?

4 Readers only ever see the faces of the asylum seekers and not those of the rescuers. Whose story do the creators want readers to focus on? Explain your answer.

5 The following pages in this graphic novel, depict the hope raised by the arrival of the helicopter being undercut by the tragic consequences of panicking asylum seekers falling overboard. (Be aware that you may find some of the images distressing if you read ahead.) What do you think the creators are suggesting about the asylum seekers' situation?

Digital narrative

Digital **narratives** harness the advantages of technology to create immersive and interactive storytelling experiences. Combining elements of traditional storytelling with digital design elements, audio and interactivity, they are an exciting contemporary form of narrative in which the reader is an active participant.

narrative The selection and sequencing of events or experiences, real or imagined, to tell a story to entertain, engage, inform and extend imagination, typically using an orientation, complication and resolution

The Boat is an award-winning digital graphic novel based on a short story by Nam Le. It was adapted by Matt Huynh for the Australian broadcaster SBS. It follows the story of Mai, a 16-year-old refugee from Vietnam, who was sent alone to Australia by her parents after the fall of Saigon. It was produced in 2015 in recognition of the 40 years since Australia first welcomed refugees from the Vietnam War.

Scan the QR code and work your way through chapter 1 of *The Boat*.

8.4 Check for understanding

1 Use a dictionary to find definitions for the following words.

a apertures: ______

b gunwale: ______

c writhing: ______

d impelling: ______

e impassive: ______

f incense: ______

g lulling: ______

2 *The Boat* begins in *medias res* (in the middle of the action). Why do you think Matt Huynh starts with the scene of a fierce storm?

______

______

3 List five ways in which Huynh creates a sense of the chaos of the storm.

______

______

______

______

______

4 Examine one of the illustrations of the refugees' bodies being tossed about inside the boat. What does this abstract (non-literal) style of illustration suggest?

5 Examine the sequence of four images of Mai seated and forcing herself to concentrate, ending with focusing on 'the contact of flesh pressed against her on every side'.

a What is suggested by the blurring of the background in each successive image?

b What do you notice about the detail in the illustration of Mai in each image?

c What do you think Huynh is trying to suggest through these techniques?

6 At one point, readers can click on an arrow that takes them into Mai's thoughts.

a Why do you think Huynh invites readers to 'step out' of the main narrative at this point?

b What effect is created by incorporating photographs of Mai's family as well as the illustrations?

c Why do you think Huynh layers images and text over the top of the photographs?

7 Explore the rest of *The Boat*. (Be aware that some parts of the story may be distressing.) Following your reading, explain what Huynh seems to be communicating about the following ideas:

a the nature of the refugee experience

b the importance of family

______

______

c Australia's decision to welcome Vietnamese refugees in 1975

______

______

8 Pick a scene you found particularly effective in communicating one of these ideas. Explain how it is constructed and why you found it effective. Use evidence to support your explanation.

______

______

______

______

______

Technological innovations

Creators of digital graphic novels have several technological innovations and advantages at their disposal compared with creators of traditional print graphic novels. Some of these are listed below.

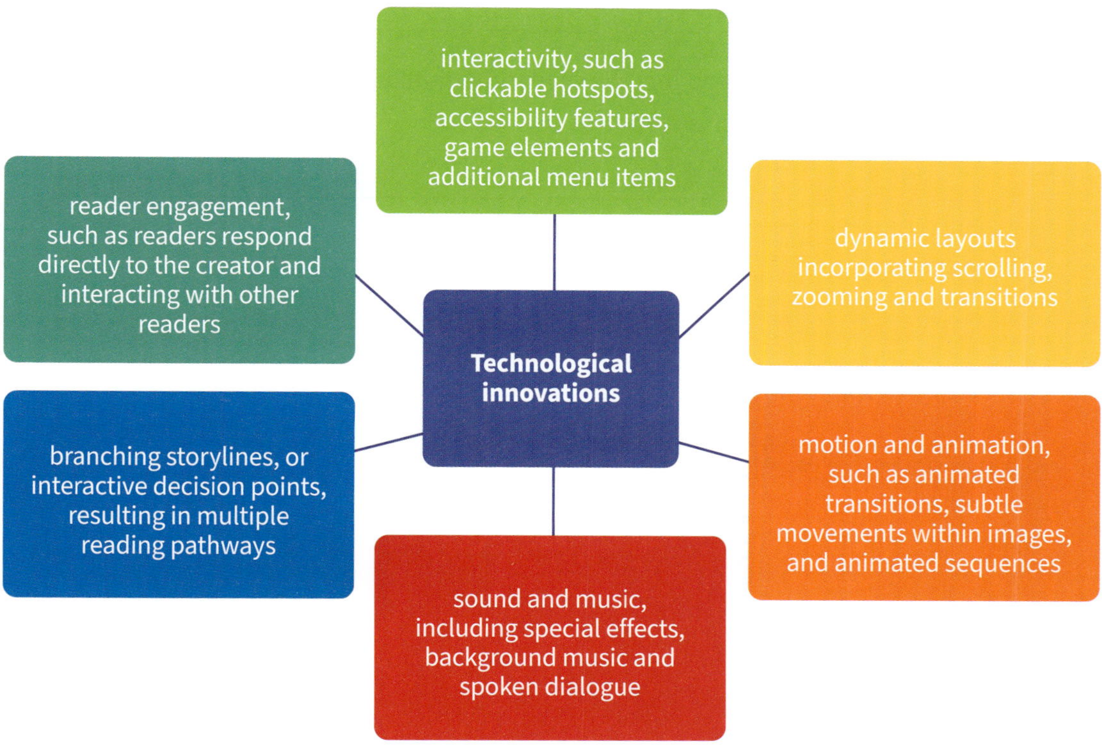

8.5 Check for understanding

1 In *The Boat*, Huynh takes advantage of the flexibility of the digital medium in many ways. Identify an example of each of the following techniques:

a sound effects: ______

b music: ______

c lighting effects: ______

d motion: ______

e animation: ______

f branching storyline: ______

2 In what ways is the site interactive; that is, how does the reader get to direct their own experience of the text?

______

______

______

3 How does your experience of reading *The Boat* compare with reading a traditional graphic novel such as *Illegal*?

______

______

______

4 List three ways in which you feel the digital medium enhances or distracts from the account of Mai's experience.

______

______

______

5 Do you feel that *The Boat* was more or less effective than *Illegal* at providing an insight into the refugee experience? Explain your answer using evidence from the texts.

____

____

____

____

____

What do we mean by 'aesthetics'?

The word '**aesthetics**' refers to the nature of beauty and art. We all have different tastes when it comes to texts, and we respond differently to texts as a result. Our aesthetic appreciation of a text incorporates the sensory and emotional experience that we have when we engage with it, as well as our recognition of its artistic qualities and style.

aesthetic Concerned with a sense of beauty or an appreciation of artistic expression

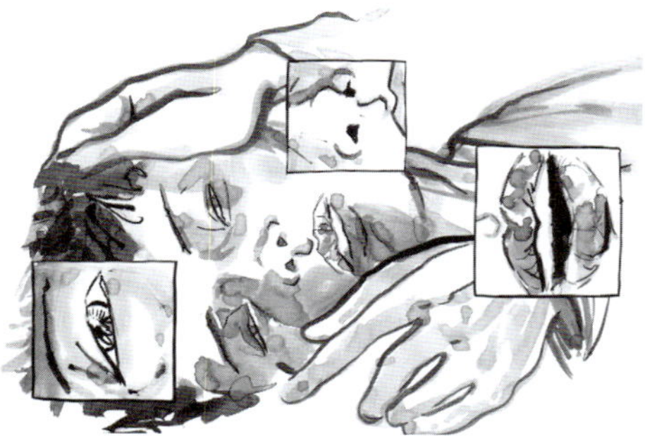

Here are some descriptions of the styles of the two graphic novels you have been looking at.

- *The Boat* uses largely monochromatic (one-colour) ink drawings which are sometimes quite realistically representational and at other times more impressionistic or abstract. They range from fine lines to broad, paintbrush-like strokes. Although Huynh sometimes uses traditional panels associated with graphic novels, at other times the text and illustrations float against the backdrop. The digital medium allows for interactive elements and the addition of sound, lighting effects and motion to complement the illustrations.
- *Illegal* uses full-colour illustrations that are clearly representational and, while somewhat cartoonish, remain quite realistic. Rigano uses different colour palettes to invite comparisons between the two epic journeys made by Ebo, across the desert and the sea. He switches between multiple panels on a page, full pages and double-page spreads to emphasise key scenes.

8.6 Reflecting and discussing

Discuss the following questions in pairs, in small groups or with the whole class as directed by your teacher.

1 *Illegal* and *The Boat* both explore the refugee experience. What similarities and differences do you notice in how the composers of the two texts have chosen to depict this experience?

2 Which style of illustration did you prefer and why?

3 Which text did you find more emotionally affecting? What emotions did you feel? What was it about this text that made you react more strongly?

4 Did you feel that one text was more aesthetically appealing than the other? What are your reasons?

8.7 Get creative

Develop a 'pitch' to encourage SBS to adapt a graphic novel you have enjoyed reading into an interactive digital graphic novel like *The Boat*.

Your pitch should include:

- the title, authors and illustrators, and genre of your graphic novel
- a brief discussion of its key ideas
- an explanation of why you think it is worthy of being adapted into a digital graphic novel; you might consider why its messages would be important or relevant to an Australian **audience**
- the aesthetic appeal of your graphic novel and why you think its style is suited to digital adaptation
- a description of a sample adapted scene, outlining some of the digital features that could be used to enhance the impact such as sound, motion or interactive elements; if you are familiar with editing software, you might even like to try to create your own sample scene.

Create a PowerPoint presentation to support your pitch and deliver it to a small group or your whole class. Afterwards, have a debate or conduct a vote on which adaptation deserves to be made by SBS.

audience An intended or assumed group of readers, listeners or viewers that a writer, designer, filmmaker or speaker is addressing

UNIT 9

Writing for the workplace

Getting your first job is an exciting milestone. Some people are lucky enough to be offered positions working with family or friends, but most people will need to formally apply for a job. Potential employers begin to evaluate an applicant's suitability for a job from the moment they start reading their application. That's why it is so important to make a great first impression! Reading job advertisements critically and using language effectively to construct professional and persuasive applications are essential skills, whether you are looking for paid work, a volunteering opportunity or work experience.

In this unit, you will learn:

- how to interpret job advertisements
- how to write cover letters and resumes
- about email etiquette.

Curriculum content

Australian Curriculum content description	Content code
Understand how language can have inclusive and exclusive social effects, and can empower or disempower people.	AC9E10LA01
Analyse text structures and language features and evaluate their effectiveness in achieving their purpose.	AC9E10LA03
Analyse and evaluate how authors organise ideas in texts to achieve a purpose.	AC9E10LY04
Plan, create, edit and publish written and multimodal texts, organising, expanding and developing ideas through experimenting with text structures, language features, literary devices and multimodal features for specific purposes and audiences in ways that may be imaginative, reflective, informative, persuasive, analytical and/or critical.	AC9E10LY06

Reading job advertisements

Job advertisements can be found in the employment pages of newspapers, through job search websites and on the websites of organisations. Many organisations also use social media platforms to recruit new employees.

Read the following advertisement from a job search website.

Position: Junior Kitchenhand

Company: Hearth & Haven

Location: Mornington, Victoria

Hearth & Haven, a popular and bustling local restaurant renowned for its exceptional food and warm atmosphere, is seeking a reliable and enthusiastic Junior Kitchenhand to join our dedicated team. If you have a passion for food, thrive in a fast-paced environment and enjoy contributing to the creation of delicious meals, this is a fantastic opportunity to be part of the Hearth & Haven family.

Responsibilities:

- Assist the chefs and kitchen staff in food preparation.
- Maintain cleanliness and organisation in the kitchen by washing dishes and undertaking general cleaning duties.
- Support the chefs in the assembly and plating of dishes.
- Help with the restocking and rotation of ingredients and supplies.
- Adhere to food safety and hygiene standards.
- Collaborate with team members to ensure smooth kitchen operations.
- Assist in the cleaning and maintenance of kitchen equipment.

Requirements:

- Strong work ethic and the ability to work efficiently in a fast-paced environment.
- Excellent communication skills and the ability to work collaboratively with a diverse team.
- Attention to detail and the ability to follow instructions accurately.
- Basic knowledge of food safety and hygiene practices, preferably a Food Handling Certificate, or a willingness to undertake this training.
- Physical stamina and the ability to stand for extended periods and lift heavy items when required.
- Flexibility in working hours, including evenings, weekends and public holidays.
- Experience preferred but training will be provided.

Benefits:

- Opportunity to work in a vibrant and friendly restaurant environment.
- Training and mentorship provided to enhance your skills and expand your culinary knowledge.
- Competitive hourly wage based on experience and performance.

- Staff meals provided during working hours.
- Potential for growth and advancement within the restaurant.
- Fun and friendly work environment.

Application Instructions:

To apply for the Junior Kitchenhand position at Hearth & Haven, please email your resume and a brief cover letter explaining your interest in the role to careers@hearthandhaven.com

For further information, contact the Manager, Carole Robertson, on 1111 222 0404.

Application Deadline: 31 August 2024

Hearth & Haven is an equal opportunity employer. We value diversity and encourage individuals from all backgrounds to apply.

9.1

Check for understanding

1 The restaurant is called Hearth & Haven.

a What do these two words mean?

Hearth: ______________________________

Haven: ______________________________

b What image of the restaurant does its name project? ______________

____

2 The advertisement includes three main subheadings to organise much of the information it includes. Define the sort of information provided within each section.

Responsibilities: ______________________________

Requirements: ______________________________

Benefits: ______________________________

3 Highlight the words in the advertisement that describe the environment or culture at Hearth & Haven.

4 Aside from those specifically listed, what sorts of qualities or traits do you think an applicant should demonstrate to show that they would be a good fit for this business?

____

____

5 What two documents do you need to supply to apply for this position?

6 The advertisement states that Hearth & Haven is offering a 'competitive hourly wage based on experience and performance'. What does this mean?

7 What is 'an equal opportunity employer'?

8 List three questions that you might ask Carole Robertson if you wanted more information before applying.

Job applications

The format and requirements for job applications can vary significantly. Some organisations will ask you to fill in an online or hard-copy form, while others will ask for a cover letter and/or resume. Sometimes, you will need to supply all three!

For professional or more senior positions, you may also be asked to write a statement addressing specific selection criteria, or to submit a curriculum vitae (CV), which is a more thoroughly detailed version of a resume.

It is important to know how to craft a successful cover letter and simple resume.

The cover letter

A cover letter is a formal letter that accompanies your resume in a job application. It introduces you to the employer, highlights your qualifications and experiences, and explains why you are the right person for the position. Think of it as your chance to make a strong first impression and convince the employer to consider you the top candidate for the job.

A good cover letter is characterised by professional, concise and persuasive language. When writing a cover letter, you should include the following language features:

Here is an example of a cover letter applying for the Junior Kitchenhand job at Hearth & Haven.

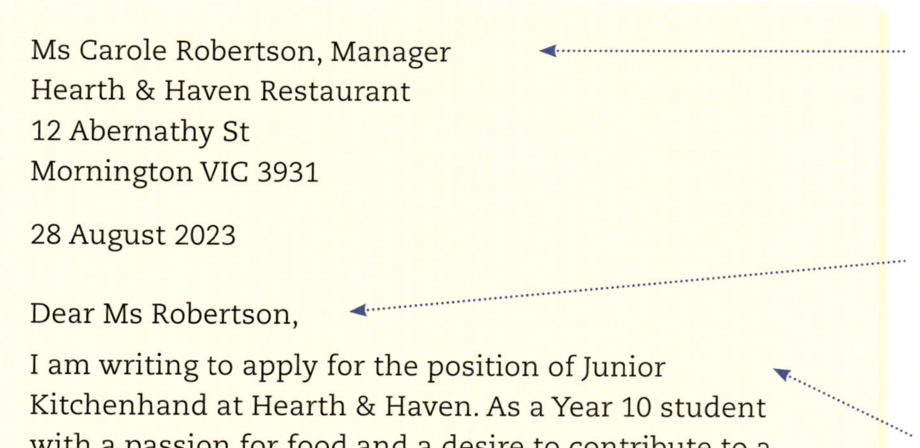

Ms Carole Robertson, Manager
Hearth & Haven Restaurant
12 Abernathy St
Mornington VIC 3931

28 August 2023

Dear Ms Robertson,

I am writing to apply for the position of Junior Kitchenhand at Hearth & Haven. As a Year 10 student with a passion for food and a desire to contribute to a bustling restaurant environment, I am excited about the opportunity to be part of the Hearth & Haven family.

I have a strong work ethic and thrive in fast-paced environments. I understand the importance of teamwork and possess excellent communication skills, allowing me to collaborate effectively with diverse team members.

Include the name and address of the recipient. You may have to find this out.

Address the hirer by name, if known.

In the first paragraph, state the job you are applying for and why you are interested.

Attention to detail is one of my strengths, and I am aware of the importance of following instructions accurately. I have demonstrated these skills throughout my experience at the Mornington Animal Shelter, working effectively with a team of both staff and volunteers to ensure that the needs of rescue animals are met in a timely and positive manner.

Although I may not have professional experience, I am eager to learn. As I am currently undertaking VCE Food Studies, I have a basic knowledge of food safety and hygiene practices. This has proved beneficial, as I regularly staff the sausage sizzle at a local sporting club, where I have put in place strategies to improve food handling conditions. I am also willing to undertake any necessary training, including obtaining a Food Handling Certificate, to enhance my skills in this role. Furthermore, my physical stamina and flexibility in working hours make me well suited to handle the demands of a kitchen environment.

I am drawn to Hearth & Haven for its warm and welcoming atmosphere, which I have experienced firsthand during my visits with my family. With my outgoing and friendly personality, I believe that I would seamlessly fit into the team. I hope to pursue a career in the food industry, and I am especially interested in the opportunities for growth and advancement within your restaurant. I am eager to contribute to the kitchen team, expand my culinary knowledge and develop my skills under the mentorship of your staff.

Thank you for considering my application. I have attached my resume for your review and would be grateful for the opportunity to discuss my suitability for the position further. Please feel free to contact me on 03 1111 4321 or braydon@greenefamily.com.au. I look forward to the possibility of joining Hearth & Haven and contributing to its continued success.

Sincerely,

Braydon Greene

Braydon Greene

In the body paragraphs, address the requirements in the advertisement and include brief, specific examples to show that you have the appropriate or required skills and attributes.

Conclude by thanking the hirer for considering your application and expressing willingness to attend an interview. Provide contact details and refer them to your resume.

Sign off with your full name and signature.

9.2

Check for understanding

1 Write down three examples from the letter of **clauses** or sentences written in the active voice (where the subject is the 'doer' of the action).

____

____

____

2 What three specific examples does Braydon provide to show that he has relevant experience?

____

____

____

3 Highlight five examples in the letter where Braydon clearly references language from the advertisement.

4 Write down two examples from the letter where Braydon is courteous to Carole Robertson in his language.

____

____

5 The job advertisement listed seven 'Requirements' for the successful application. Do you think Braydon successfully addresses each of these? Explain your answer.

____

____

____

6 On a scale of 1–5, with 5 being the highest, how would you rate the confidence and enthusiasm of Braydon's **tone**? Give three reasons for your rating.

____

____

____

7 Using a different colour from before, highlight five examples of positive language in the letter.

8 How would you describe Braydon's character or personality based on this letter?

9 At one point, Braydon writes, 'I hope to pursue a career in the food industry'. What would be a stronger word than 'hope' in this **context**? Circle the best answer.

want intend wish desire

10 Overall, do you feel that this is a successful cover letter? Explain your reasoning.

11 The following paragraph is from another application. Rewrite it in more formal language.

So, I saw your ad for that kitchenhand gig at Hearth & Haven, and I think I would be good for the job. I don't have that much experience, but I figure you will be able to teach me. I mean, I've helped out with some cooking stuff at home and sometimes I work at my uncle's kebab shop when he's really short-staffed, so I kinda know my way around the kitchen. I'm a chill person, and I reckon I can handle the workload.

clause A grammatical unit referring to a happening or state, e.g. 'the team won' (happening), 'the dog is red' (state), usually containing a subject and a verb group/phrase
tone The mood created by the language features used by an author and the way the text makes the reader feel
context An environment or situation (social, cultural or historical) in which a text is responded to or created. Or wording surrounding an unfamiliar word, which a reader or listener uses to understand its meaning

The resume

A resume is a concise document that summarises your education, work experience, skills and achievements. It provides potential employers with a concise overview of your qualifications and suitability for a job. You should think of it as a marketing tool that showcases your qualities and highlights the value you can bring to a prospective employer.

Read this resume prepared by another student who wants to apply for the job at Hearth & Haven.

Resume of Gamina Singh

Address: 23 Arbory Ave, Forestville VIC 3333
Phone: 0123 456 789
Email: gaminas@jmail.com

Provide clear contact details.

Objective: As a motivated and hard-working Year 11 student at Arbory State School with a passion for teamwork and helping others, I am seeking part-time opportunities to gain further experience in the food industry.

An objective can make your context and purpose clear to a potential employer.

Education

Include a list of your most recent and relevant education and work experiences, listing key outcomes and duties.

Arbory State School, current Year 11 VCE student
Excellent academic performance, particularly in the sciences
Expected graduation year: 2024

Access Australia Training, 2022
Completed Food Handling Certificate

Work Experience

Bert's Ice-Cream Kiosk, November 2022 to February 2023

- Assisted customers in a fast-paced environment, providing excellent service and ensuring customer satisfaction
- Handled cash transactions and maintained accurate cash register records
- Prepared and served a variety of ice-cream treats, ensuring high standards of food hygiene and safety

Use subheadings, bullet points and concise language.

Acacia Care Home, September 2022 (School-Based Work Experience)

- Interacted with residents, providing companionship and assisting with daily activities
- Supported care staff in maintaining a clean and organised environment
- Developed strong communication and empathy skills while working with elderly individuals

Extracurricular Activities

Drama Club

- Actively participated in rehearsals and performances, demonstrating reliability, creativity and teamwork
- Developed skills in improvisation, character development and stage presence

Netball Team

- Collaborated with team members to achieve common goals and improve skills
- Demonstrated commitment, discipline and leadership while participating in regular training sessions and competitive matches

Skills

Excellent communication and interpersonal skills
Strong teamwork and collaboration abilities
Ability to manage multiple commitments effectively
Initiative, drive and strong work ethic

Achievements

Various academic achievement awards in Science
Fairest and Best trophy for 2021 Netball season

References

Robert Drang, Owner
Bert's Ice-Cream Kiosk
Ph: 1111 543 210

Mala Goldsworth
Drama Teacher, Arbory State School
Ph: 1111 432 109

Include additional experiences, such as volunteering, associations or interesting opportunities in which you developed valuable skills.

Summarise your positive qualities and achievements.

Include at least one referee who can confirm your experiences and attributes.

9.3 Check for understanding

1 Highlight the strong verbs used by Gamina in her resume when listing her experience.

2 How would you characterise the language used by Gamina in her resume? Circle the most appropriate adjectives from the following list.

verbose	descriptive	succinct	direct
clear	action-oriented	professional	informal
conversational	detailed	positive	poetic

3 Why do you think Gamina included her Drama Club and Netball Team experience? What qualities do these activities demonstrate that might be valuable for this job?

____

____

4 What qualities do you think each of Gamina's referees would be able to confirm for a future employer?

a Robert Drang: ______________________________

b Mala Goldsworth: ____________________________

5 Using a different colour, highlight three areas where Gamina has tailored her resume to suit the job advertisement for Hearth & Haven.

6 What four qualities does Gamina describe herself as having in her 'Objective'?

____________________ ____________________

____________________ ____________________

7 Do you think the rest of Gamina's resume provides evidence of these qualities? Explain your answer.

____

____

____

8 If you were Carole Robertson, the manager of Hearth & Haven, what are three questions that you would want to ask Gamina to see whether she is the best candidate for the advertised job?

____

____

____

9.4 Reflecting and discussing

Discuss the following questions in pairs, in small groups or with the whole class as directed by your teacher.

1 Based on the cover letter and resume you have read, what skills and qualities does each of the applicants, Braydon and Gamina, have that would make them suited to the job of Junior Kitchenhand at Hearth & Haven?

2 Which of the two applicants would you employ? What are the reasons for your choice?

3 Role-play an interview between Ms Robertson and either Braydon or Gamina. Use the information from the job advertisement to predict six questions that Ms Robertson might ask.

Email etiquette

In many work situations, including when applying for a job, you will communicate via email. It is essential that you use appropriate etiquette (conventions of polite and respectful behaviour), especially when communicating with people who are senior to you or whom you haven't met.

» Use a professional-sounding email address.

» Include a clear and concise subject line to let people know the **purpose** of your email.

» Greet the recipient appropriately (e.g. 'Dear [name]' or 'Good morning, [name]'). Generally, you should use their title and surname (e.g. Ms Robertson) until invited to do otherwise.

» Maintain a professional tone.

» Use formal and correct English.

» Be concise: emails are intended to be a short form of communication. You might politely inquire whether the recipient is well, wish them a good day, or offer another similar courtesy, but keep the body of your email focused on your purpose.

» Proofread your email carefully before sending.

» Double-check the addresses of your recipients before sending.

purpose An intended or assumed reason for a type of text

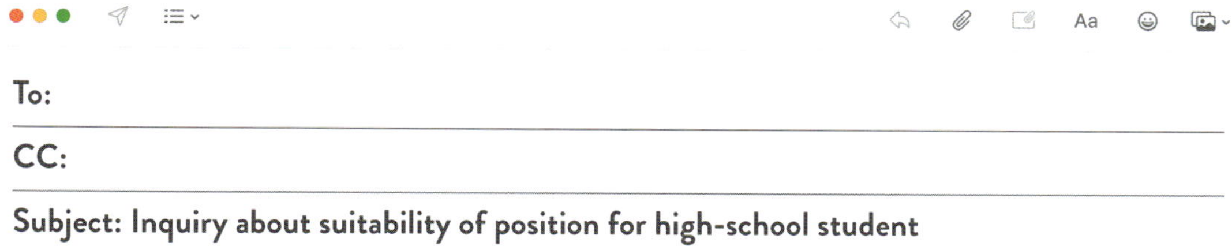

Dear Ms Robertson,

I hope this email finds you well. I am writing to inquire about the Junior Kitchenhand position at Hearth & Haven. I am a high-school student currently studying at Flinders College, and I am interested in applying for the position if it is suitable for someone in my circumstances.

I am eager to find part-time employment within the restaurant industry and would welcome any information you can provide regarding the suitability of this position for a high-school student like myself. If it is appropriate, I would be delighted to submit an application and further discuss my experience and availability.

Thank you for your time and consideration. I look forward to your response.

Kind regards,

Andrew Pizzano

9.5 Get creative

Using the information gleaned from Gamina's resume, write an appropriate cover letter from Gamina applying for the Junior Kitchenhand position at Hearth & Haven. Alternatively, search online for a job that you would find interesting and that is appropriate for your context and experience. Write a cover letter that *you* might send if you were to apply for this job.

1 Use Braydon's cover letter as a model. Make sure you follow the appropriate **conventions**.
2 Keep your language professional, positive, action-focused, clear and concise.
3 Proofread the letter carefully, checking both for errors and that you have addressed all aspects of the job advertisement.

convention An accepted practice that has developed over time and is generally used and understood (e.g. use of punctuation)

UNIT 10

Creating imaginative texts

Behind every enthralling story – from films and television shows to novels and short stories – is the work of somebody's imagination and creative process. We use our imaginations to tell stories all the time. Whether we are recounting the events of our day, telling a funny anecdote or remembering something scary, we are nearly always trying to evoke a particular idea and generate a particular response from our audience. The art of storytelling – be it truth, fiction or somewhere in between – is a skill that you can practise.

In this unit, you will learn:

- how to write for a purpose and audience
- about the elements of a narrative
- how to use paragraphs, sentence structure and punctuation for effect.

Curriculum content

Australian Curriculum content description	Content code
Understand how paragraph structure can be varied to create cohesion, and paragraphs and images can be integrated for different purposes.	AC9E10LA04
Analyse and evaluate the effectiveness of particular sentence structures to express and craft ideas.	AC9E10LA05
Understand how authors use and experiment with punctuation.	AC9E10LA09
Create and edit literary texts with a sustained 'voice', selecting and adapting text structures, literary devices, and language, auditory and visual features for purposes and audiences.	AC9E10LE08

Establishing purpose in your writing

When planning and writing your own story, it is important to identify a clear and meaningful **purpose**. This will help you not only to formulate your ideas, but also to shape your **narrative** and demonstrate a complex understanding of the ways in which language, structure and **style** can create meaning.

purpose An intended or assumed reason for a type of text
narrative The selection and sequencing of events or experiences, real or imagined, to tell a story to entertain, engage, inform and extend imagination, typically using an orientation, complication and resolution
style The distinctive language features, text structures and/or subject matter in a text which may shape meaning, be enjoyed for its aesthetic qualities or distinguish the work of an author, period etc.

10.1 Reflecting and discussing

Discuss the following questions in pairs, in small groups or with the whole class as directed by your teacher.

1 Can you recall a story that you have read that you found particularly enthralling? If your answer is yes, what was it that captured your interest? If your answer is no, why have you found the stories you've read uninteresting?

2 Think about a time when you used your imagination to create a vivid world or scenario in your mind. What sparked your creativity and allowed you to construct that imaginative space?

3 Do you have a favourite author? What aspects of their writing would you most like to be able to emulate?

There can be several purposes for writing stories. Some of these are listed below.

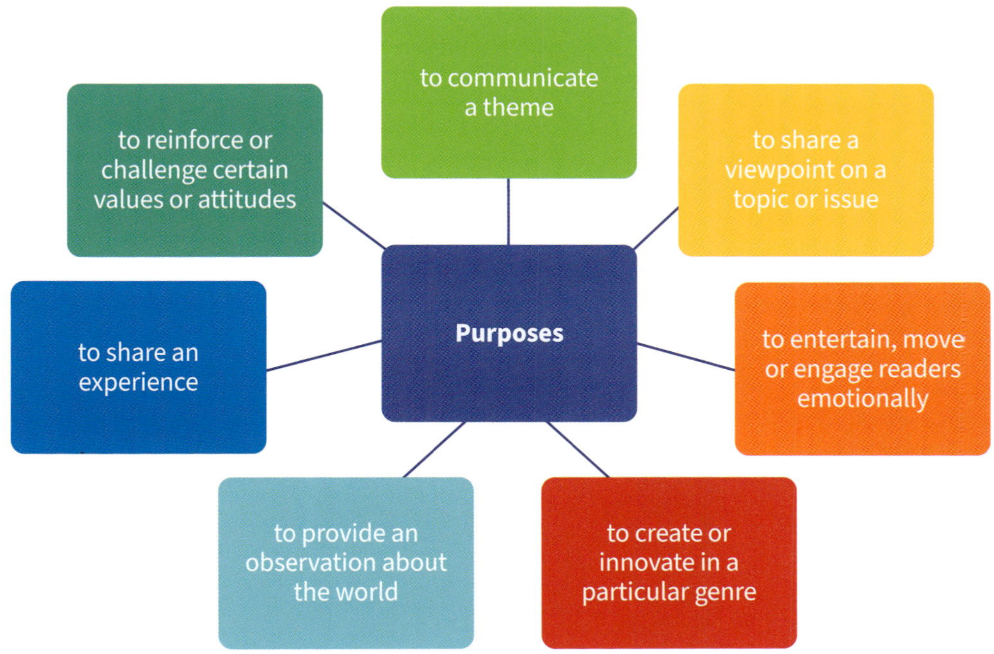

10.2 Check for understanding

In the spaces below each prompt in the table, write plans for two (of the three) narratives that would achieve the two different stated purposes. In each space, list dot points outlining the beginning, middle and end of the story.

Prompt: a long journey is interrupted by a disaster	
Purpose: to write a short narrative that conforms to the science fiction genre	Purpose: to write a short narrative that shocks the audience with a plot twist
Prompt: a group of teenagers are on a camping trip when they discover a dead body	
Purpose: to write a short narrative that challenges the crime/thriller genre	Purpose: to convey the **theme** that formative experiences shape the way we view the world
Prompt: a person who has just moved to Australia catches a bus through a town or city	
Purpose: to challenge patriotic **attitudes** that Australia is the 'lucky country'	Purpose: to reinforce Australian egalitarian **values**

theme The main idea, concept or message of a text
attitudes Particular ways of thinking and feeling towards people or things
values Ideas and beliefs specific to individuals and groups

Targeting an audience

Targeting a specific **audience** helps you to create a story that resonates with your readers. By understanding your readers' interests, preferences and experiences, you can craft characters and plots that they will relate to.

audience An intended or assumed group of readers, listeners or viewers that a writer, designer, filmmaker or speaker is addressing

Furthermore, targeting an audience helps you to convey your intended message effectively. Whether you want to communicate a moral lesson, exploring social issues or sparking the reader's imagination, knowing your audience allows you to select themes that are relevant and meaningful to them.

Choosing a protagonist

The age, gender and social profile of your **protagonist** will typically reflect the target audience of the story. Even if you are writing genre fiction, such as fantasy or science fiction, your audience should still be able to relate to your characters, even if their **context** is different. We may not all be young wizards battling dark forces, but we know what it is like to face challenges while growing up!

protagonist The main character in a text

context An environment or situation (social, cultural or historical) in which a text is responded to or created. Or wording surrounding an unfamiliar word, which a reader or listener uses to understand its meaning

For example, imagine you want to write a story that conveys the theme that it is important for teenagers to develop independence. The following table shows how you might use your protagonist to communicate this theme to two different audiences.

Audience	How would this audience shape my story?
teenagers	Fifteen-year-old Lily, accustomed to relying on her parents, faces her first summer alone. Overwhelmed at first, she gradually discovers her own strength and independence, taking on responsibilities and facing challenges. As her confidence grows, she explores new interests and learns the importance of embracing her own identity.
adults	Sarah, an overprotective mother, reluctantly leaves her teenage daughter Emma alone for a week. As Emma faces challenges and makes decisions, she discovers her capabilities and independence. Sarah realises her excessive protectiveness has hindered Emma's growth, leading to open conversations about the importance of independence.

Choosing events and conflicts

Another way of engaging your audience is by including conflicts that the audience will relate to. 'Conflict' in narrative writing refers to the problems faced by the protagonist and other characters. There are different types of conflicts, although these often interrelate.

» Internal conflict: a character might experience a moral or psychological conflict, such as agonising over a decision they need to make.

» Interpersonal conflict: conflict may occur between characters, and this could range from an argument to a physical fight or could simply be caused by one character proving to be an obstacle to what the other desires.

» External conflict: conflict can be between an individual and the wider world, such as society, the environment or even supernatural forces.

10.3

Check for understanding

1 Outline two real-life conflicts that might be encountered by each audience listed below and that you could use as premises for two stories.

a primary-school students

____

____

b high-school students

____

____

c teachers

____

____

d parents of teenagers

____

____

2 Harry has spent his childhood growing up in a rural part of Australia. However, his parents have decided that he should go and live with his grown-up sister in the city to complete his last few years of school. Identify three conflicts Harry might face in this story.

a internal: ______________________________

b interpersonal: ______________________________

c external: ______________________________

3 Explain why young adults might be able to relate to the conflicts that Harry experiences even if they have not lived in rural Australia.

____

____

Developing memorable characters

Characters are developed not just through description, but through clues that readers pick up from their speech, actions and interactions with others. Thinking about a character's motivations and goals when you are writing is an important aspect of characterisation. It helps make your characters realistic and their actions understandable.

Other important aspects of developing effective and memorable characters include:

- *developing their backstory* – give each of your characters a history. You don't neec to share it all with your readers, but reveal key details to help them understand who your characters are today.
- *giving them a unique voice* – write each character's dialogue and thoughts in a way that reflects their personality and makes them different from other characters.
- *showing not telling* – use indirect characterisation to reveal your characters' personalities through their thoughts, speech, actions and reactions, rather than simply telling your readers about them.
- *ensuring your protagonist develops* – your protagonist should grow throughout the story as a result of their experiences. A static (unchanging) main character can become boring for readers.

10.4

Check for understanding

1 Complete the following table, explaining how the character of Jonathan might respond according to each of the different motivations.

Scenario	Character motivation	How might the character respond?
Jonathan has been invited to the cinema with friends to see a highly anticipated MA15+ rated film. However, his parents are late getting home, and Jonathan's 13-year-old brother, whom he is supposed to be looking after, wants to come.	strong family values and love for his brother	
	a desire to be popular and fit in with the crowd	
	a fear of getting into trouble for leaving his brother behind	
	frustration over a responsibility that he feels is unfair	

2 Think of a character from a story you know well. Complete the following table with details about their characterisation.

What is their appearance?	How do they speak?	How do other characters typically react to them?	What motivates or drives them?	How do they change throughout the story?

3 Imagine this situation: your chosen character (from question 2) discovers a large sum of money.

a What would they do with the money?

____

____

b Why do you think they would do this?

____

____

c How would they feel about their decision?

____

____

d What consequences might arise as a result of their choice?

____

____

Narrative structure

One of the biggest components in creating a great story is developing your plot – the sequence of events that make up your story. As your protagonist encounters various conflicts, their personality will determine how they approach these problems, and the consequences of their actions will determine the next conflict to arise. As a story progresses, the stakes tend to increase, until the protagonist faces their greatest challenge, in the climax.

Traditional narrative structure includes the following five stages.

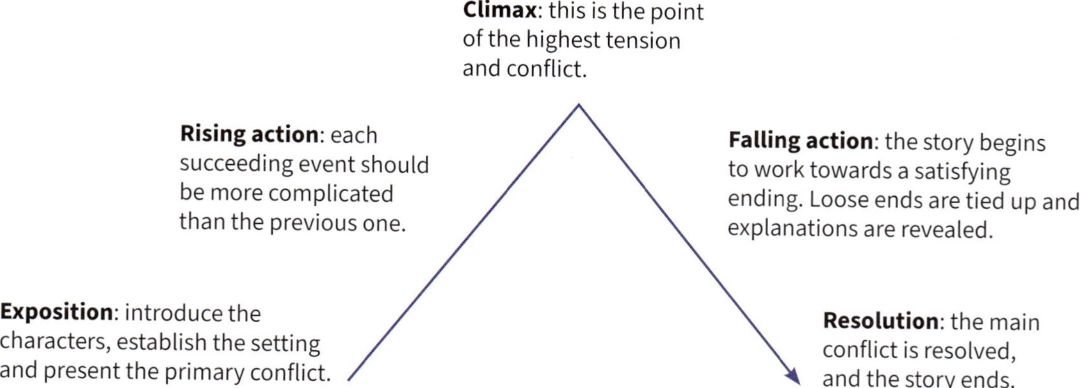

When writing your own story, you may also consider one of the following devices to add interest and intrigue.

- A *flashback* takes the audience from the present moment to a scene in the past. It helps provide background information and gives readers access to characters' memories to explain something about the story. Flashbacks can be sudden thoughts, hazy dreams or vivid memories.
- A *circular narrative* begins and ends in the same location, emphasising the knowledge gained by the protagonist throughout the story.
- A *plot twist* is an unexpected event or turn of events in a story that completely changes the direction or likely outcome of the plot. It aims to surprise the audience and challenge their expectations. Plot twists can be either totally unexpected or subtly hinted at through earlier details.
- A *cliff-hanger* is achieved when the main conflict is unresolved, placing the reader in a state of tension or uncertainty. It is important not to leave too much unresolved in a standalone story, as it may frustrate your audience.
- Beginning your story *in medias res*, or in the middle of the action, can provide a dramatic opening that engages the audience from the outset.

10.5 Check for understanding

Write a brief outline showing how you could complete this story using each of the narrative structures or structural elements listed in the table below.

Neesha is a veterinarian who moves to a small rural town where there have been persistent rumours of a mysterious creature that inhabitants the bushland. One day, just before dusk, Neesha is called to a remote farm to help an injured cow. As she tends to the cow, a pair of deep-violet eyes appears in the shadows of the bush.

traditional narrative structure	
flashback	
circular narrative	
plot twist	
in medias res	

Paragraphing in imaginative writing

The use of paragraphs in imaginative writing is an essential tool in communicating your story clearly and directing your reader. Unlike analytical writing, imaginative writing has paragraphs of widely varying lengths. Some paragraphs can be a single sentence – or even just a word or two!

New paragraphs are used:

- to transition between ideas or events
- to indicate changes in time or location – even minor transitions, such as a character moving from one room to another
- to mark each new speaker during a section of dialogue
- to emphasise something for dramatic effect
- to manipulate tension, as lengthy paragraphs slow the reader down while short paragraphs increase the pace
- to enhance readability and maintain an entertaining experience for the reader.

10.6

Check for understanding

1 Read this extract from Kate Furnivall's 2012 novel *Shadows on the Nile*. In the story, the protagonist hears her young brother scream in the middle of the night and wakes up the next morning to find him gone. Use the rules above to **edit** the text, indicating where you would choose to start each new paragraph by writing a double forward slash : '//'.

> Night noises are the worst. They are the ones that come at you out of the darkness and seize you by the throat. They are the ones that slither under the door of your bedroom. Stop it. Don't do that. Jessica rapped her knuckles against her forehead. Don't. You're too old to be frightened of nothing. Too grown up. Seven years and eight months. Jessica didn't like the dark, and she could never understand how the air could become so solid at night or why its weight was sometimes so heavy on her chest that she had to pummel her lungs to make them work. She drew her knees up to her chin and wrapped her arms around her shins, hugging her winceyette nightdress – the one with the blue ribbons – tight against her skin. Even under her bedspread she was cold. Suddenly it came again, the sound that had woken her, a whimpering that made the blonde hairs rise on the back of her neck. She threw off the quilt cover and leapt out of bed. Her heart was juddering against her bony ribs as she pushed her way through the darkness, parting it with her hands like a curtain until she reached her bedroom door. She gripped its brass knob and quickly turned it. Nothing happened. Her fingers tried again. Nothing. It was locked.

2 Compare your paragraph breaks with those of a peer. Did you choose the same places? If not, how did your peer's paragraphing change your experience of the story?

____

____

edit To prepare, alter, adapt or refine with attention to grammar, spelling, punctuation and vocabulary

Creating a voice in your writing

Voice in writing is the personality expressed in a text. It can be described using words like 'unreliable', 'aggressive', 'naive', 'observant', 'detached' and 'jovial'. Developing a specific voice for a narrator or character can greatly impact your writing and can be constructed through:

- narrative **point of view**, such as writing in first person, can create a greater sense of intimacy between the reader and the protagonist
- sentence structure and syntax, as the types of sentences used and the way they are arranged can reflect how the narrator or character thinks
- vocabulary and diction, as word choices reveal much about a narrator or character's personality, background and attitudes
- dialogue style, such as whether a character's speech is casual, verbose, quirky or accented
- figurative language, to add originality and style to the narrator or character's voice.

voice The distinct personality of a piece of writing; the individual writing style of the composer, created through the way they use and mix various language features (e.g. a narrative using a child's voice)
point of view The position from which the text is designed to be perceived (e.g. a narrator might take a role of first or third person, omniscient or restricted in knowledge of events or the opinion presented in a text)

Using figurative language

Figurative language draws comparisons to help the reader picture the scenario in a way that reflects the mood, and voice of the narrator or character.

Scenario	Narrator's voice	Example of figurative language
Akari is sitting on the grass in the sun.	frustrated and agitated	The sun hung in the sky like an unwelcome guest, its scorching rays pressing down on Akari relentlessly as if she were trapped beneath a giant magnifying glass.
	calm and peaceful	The sun bathed Akari in warmth like a cosy blanket on a winter's day, embracing her with its gentle rays and filling her with a comforting sensation.

10.7

Check for understanding

1 Write definitions for the following figurative language features:

a simile: ______

b metaphor: ______

c personification: ______

d hyperbole: ______

2 Write four sentences to suit the following scenario, using each of the above figurative language devices in turn. After each sentence, describe the voice and atmosphere you were trying to create.

Scenario	Sentence using figurative language	Voice and atmosphere
Truong gets home after a long shift at work to find the house dark and a meal left in the oven for him by his mother.		

3 Read the passage below, which describes a mother's reaction to her child's report card. Highlight the features that create the irate voice. Look for sentence structures, word choice, narrative point of view and language features.

As the report card landed on the kitchen table, Amina's heart sank. Frustration and anger swirled within her like a thunderstorm. How could Malik fail the test? All those late nights of studying, the sacrifices made for their education. A wave of disappointment surged through her veins, threatening to burst.

'Are you kidding me?' she muttered under her breath, her voice dripping with annoyance. The weight of unfulfilled expectations bore down on her, the dreams of her child's success now shrouded in doubt. She struggled to keep her composure, but her eyes betrayed the storm of emotions raging inside her.

4 Rewrite this passage so that Amina's voice is empathetic and concerned.

____

____

____

____

____

____

____

____

Manipulating sentence structure

Writers often manipulate sentence structure to create certain effects. Sometimes, they break the usual rules of grammar in order to do so. There are many ways in which you can manipulate sentence structure to add impact to your writing, some of which are outlined in the following table. (You might also like to review the information about sentence structure in Unit 7.)

Technique	Examples	Effect
using a verbless clause – a sentence structure that doesn't have a main verb or 'doing' word	'What about the other woman? With the dark glasses and briefcase?' 'Jaime ran for the doorway. When I got there, I saw him.'	draws attention to the character or subject and adds impact or detail to the description
placing a coordinating conjunction like 'and', 'but' or 'or' at the beginning of a sentence	'And little did she know that life would never be the same again for the reality was that he wasn't telling the truth.'	emphasises the information that follows or highlights a continuation or contradiction of the previous statement

Technique	Examples	Effect
using informal grammar and elision (blending words together)	'So I said to him – you're gonna love this – I said to him, "Mate, what do you think you're doing?" and he was like, "I dunno, I just woke up here" and then Crakey ... Hey Crakey, what'd you say to that fella?'	mimics the irregularity of vernacular speech patterns
using an ellipsis (...) within or at the end of a sentence	'Aria stepped into the dark room, her heart pounding, and then ... everything went quiet.'	indicates an unfinished thought or trailing off, or suggests a pause to create a sense of mystery or tension
using a dash (–) at the end of a sentence	If you're not sure what to order, look at the ingredients—they can help you decide on the nutritional value.	indicates an abrupt interruption or a sudden shift in thought

10.8 Check for understanding

Rewrite the following passage using some of the techniques discussed above to add impact and interest. You can also insert additional words.

> I was rowing my small boat on the lake with a light breeze behind me. Gentle waves lapped the boat, and the sky above was a calm blue. A sudden chill tickled my neck, and I shivered, looking over my shoulder. Dark clouds had appeared on the horizon, their shadows reaching out over the water. The once gentle waves began to turn rough, sending up a fierce spray as the wind intensified. The water became a dull steel grey. Fear gripped me as I hurriedly rowed back to shore, struggling against the growing waves, hoping to reach safety before the storm unleashed its full force.

Active and passive voice

The difference between active and passive voice lies in how the **subject** and object of a sentence are positioned and emphasised.

subject A word or group of words (usually a noun group/phrase) in a sentence or clause representing the person, thing or idea doing the action that follows (e.g. 'The dog [subject] was barking')

In *active voice*, the subject of the sentence performs the action. For example: 'John [subject] threw [action] the ball [object].'

In *passive voice*, the subject receives the action. For example: 'The ball [subject] was thrown [action] by John [agent].'

Use active voice to:	Use passive voice to:
› emphasise the subject as the doer of the action › make your writing more direct, concise and engaging › clearly attribute responsibility or credit to a specific person or entity › maintain a sense of energy and momentum in your writing.	› intentionally omit the doer of the action › shift the focus from the subject to the object of the action › maintain a more formal or impersonal **tone** › emphasise the action itself rather than the doer.

tone The mood created by the language features used by an author and the way the text makes the reader feel

10.9 Check for understanding

Change the following examples of active voice into passive voice or vice versa as needed. One example has been done for you.

Active voice	Passive voice
Ali picked up the pile of papers.	The pile of papers was picked up by Ali.
	The broken car was fixed by the mechanic.
Joanne slowly pushed the door open.	
	The ball was chased across the field by the dog.

Punctuating dialogue

When writing dialogue, remember these important rules.

Rule	Example
Use speech marks to indicate words that are spoken aloud.	'Hey, Bruna,' he called out.
Keep punctuation inside the quotation marks, typically using a comma to separate the dialogue from the dialogue tag.	'Hello,' said Marcelo, 'how are you?'
Use an ellipsis to show hesitation.	'The reason I wanted to talk to you, Bruna, is to ask you ...'
Use a dash to show that somebody was interrupted.	'The reason I wanted to talk to you, Bruna, is to ask you –' 'Bruna,' yelled Mum, 'come here please.'
Include actions and gestures to reveal emotions.	'I'm sorry.' He stepped closer. 'The truth is that the more I think about it, the more I realise this isn't going to work.' He reached out to place a hand on her shoulder.
Vary your dialogue tags.	'You mean the more you speak with your mother,' Bruna sneered.
Get creative and experiment with punctuation to indicate emotion.	'You ... Y-you leave my mother out of this!' Marcelo's face turned a distinctive shade of red.

10.10 Check for understanding

In your English notebook, write a conversation between two characters who play for the same football team. They are good friends but fierce rivals. They meet up, planning to talk about a party they are attending on the weekend, but during the conversation one reveals that they have been selected as team captain over the other. Use the rules above and include some actions to support the dialogue. Use the space below to plan the conversation.

____

____

____

____

____

____

10.11 Get creative

Demonstrate your understanding of voice. Write two connected imaginative texts: they should both describe the same incident that leads to conflict, but each must be narrated by a different character. Each text should be written in the first person, should be roughly 400 words long and should portray the conflict as it is experienced by its narrator.

Follow the steps below, using your English notebook to record your responses.

1. What is your central idea? Choose a topic that you want to explore in your texts. It should be broad enough to allow for different **perspectives** and voices. It might be something like family, friendships, school or sport.
2. Within your central idea, imagine a situation in which two different people might interact and an incident that might lead to conflict. For example, a dinner might bring estranged family members together, or a sportsperson might arrive late to training.
3. Create two characters who might respond differently to the incident. What conflicts would it create for them? What might they be motivated by?
4. Brainstorm a range of voices you could use to depict your two characters. Think about their personalities, ages, backgrounds, cultural perspectives and viewpoints. Select two voices that contrast strongly with each other.
5. Plan your two texts. Outline their structure and organisation. Your two characters should describe the same incident from their contrasting points of view. You could use a different tense for each character and describe the incident from beforehand, as it takes place or afterwards. You should not write a whole narrative here: just two key scenes.
6. Draft your texts. For each one, immerse yourself in the mindset of the central character. Consider their unique vocabulary, ways of speaking and personality. Allow the voice of each character to guide your writing choices.
7. Review and edit the first drafts of your texts. Look for areas where the voice could be strengthened or made more authentic. Pay attention to the consistency of the voice throughout each text. Make adjustments to vocabulary, sentence structure and tone as needed. Write out a second draft of each text.
8. Polish the second drafts of your texts. Pay attention to areas where the voices could be further developed or made more distinct. Refine the language, tone and style to enhance the impact of the texts.

perspective A lens through which the author perceives the world and creates a text, or the lens through which the reader or viewer perceives the world and understands a text

UNIT 11

Using comprehension strategies

Every day, you come across a range of texts that you will need to comprehend. To 'comprehend' something means to understand and make meaning from it. These texts that you are required to understand might include an advertisement on television, a recipe for dinner, a train timetable, an explanation in a textbook, a webpage, a chapter of a novel, or the feed on a social media site. Clearly, comprehension plays a vital role in all of our lives on a daily basis. Well-developed comprehension skills allow us to function easily rather than living in a state of complete confusion.

In this unit, you will learn:

- about different comprehension strategies
- to use different comprehension strategies for a range of text forms
- to use comprehension strategies to enhance your understanding and enjoyment of texts.

Curriculum content

Australian Curriculum content description	Content code
Analyse and evaluate how people, places, events and concepts are represented in texts and reflect contexts.	AC9E10LY01
Integrate comprehension strategies such as visualising, predicting, connecting, summarising, monitoring, questioning and inferring to analyse and interpret complex and abstract ideas.	AC9E10LY05

What are comprehension strategies?

Comprehension strategies are the specific processes we use to make sense of texts so that we can understand them. This unit will particularly draw your attention to the following comprehension skills:

comprehension strategies Processes used by readers to make meaning from texts. They include activating and using prior knowledge, predicting likely future events in a text, monitoring meaning and critically reflecting

Each of these strategies is explained separately below. However, it is important to remember that often you will use more than one strategy at the same time to comprehend a text. Indeed, the Check for understanding and Reflecting and discussing activities throughout Units 1–10 of this book integrate a range of different comprehension strategies simultaneously.

In this unit, the comprehension strategies that are a particular focus in each section are indicated before the activities commence. This will help you to be aware of the specific processes you are using in each activity.

Summary of common comprehension strategies

Skimming is reading quickly in order to get a general overview of a text. It only allows for an overall impression of the text but is a very useful strategy in helping you decide what kind of text you are reading and identifying its main topic.

Scanning involves reading quickly in order to find specific facts, words or phrases. This strategy requires you to move your eyes quickly down the text to find only the information that will answer a particular question.

Activating prior knowledge requires you to think about what you already know to help you understand a new text. It may involve brainstorming what you already know about a text's main topic or making connections with something similar you have already read.

Visualising involves forming a mental image or picture in your head to illustrate what you are reading.

Predicting involves making a logical presumption about what might happen next in a text, often based on prior experience of similar texts.

Connecting is about making links between the text you are trying to understand and other texts. It also involves thinking about how the text relates to you and to the world at large.

Summarising involves choosing only the most important information in a text and then rewriting it in shortened form.

Questioning refers to asking yourself questions before, during or after reading a text in ways that help you think more deeply about what you are reading and help clarify your understanding.

Inferring means making a deduction about what something might mean. Even though a text might not state something specifically, you will be able to draw logical conclusions based on the clues or hints it offers and through your skills of reasoning.

Comprehension focus 1: scanning, summarising and inferring

The following extract is from an online article written by Sarthak Mondal about Manchester City being crowned Premier League champions. It was published in *The Conversation.*

Manchester City: how Pep Guardiola's leadership style formed a squad of champions

Published: May 31, 2023 5.11pm AEST
Author: Sarthak Mondal

As the final whistle blew in Nottingham Forest's 1–0 win over Arsenal on May 20, celebrations erupted approximately 85 miles away in the city of Manchester. Thanks to the points Arsenal lost in their defeat, Manchester City were crowned Premier League champions for the third consecutive year – and for the fifth time in the last six seasons.

Arsenal were leading the league at the halfway stage, but it's not unusual for Manchester City to turn the heat up in the second half of the season. They did so before in 2018/2019, beating Liverpool to the title on the final day.

Two elements have been crucial to Manchester City's sustained success – the depth and ability of the squad and manager Pep Guardiola's leadership style.

Manchester City's squad depth (the quality of all their signed players, not just the starting 11) can be attributed to their transfer activity over the past three seasons. The club has one of the highest net spends in the division, but it was their strategic spending – acquiring players who would fit Guardiola's plans for the team – that enabled their success.

While the squad already had long-serving, high-performing players such as midfielder Kevin De Bruyne (2015), after Guardiola's takeover in 2016, adequate cover for the first team was acquired in the form of Kalvin Phillips, Sergio Gomez and Manuel Akanji.

This means Guardiola has enough quality players to form almost two different starting 11s without sacrificing the calibre of players and playing style. This is something their rivals, Arsenal, did not possess.

There is fierce competition between clubs to access and develop global top talent.

To keep up, many are looking for alternative solutions.

One dominant approach is called vertical integration. This is where some club owners – such as City Football Group (CFG), which owns Man City, and Red Bull Sport – acquire satellite clubs in smaller leagues. These smaller or affiliated clubs are then owned or controlled by the main club or organisation. The aim is to secure playing time for young talents who would otherwise be blocked from getting first team opportunities.

CFG owns satellite clubs in 10 countries, including the US, Japan, Australia and India. Manchester City uses the scouting network of these satellite clubs to learn of players that wouldn't otherwise be on their radar. They then bring them into the CFG family offering a possible future of playing in the Manchester City first team.

This gives City a competitive advantage over their rivals in England's 'Big Six' clubs, as none of their competitors have this kind of multi-club ownership model.

Leadership style

Guardiola has created a powerful identity at Manchester City. His leadership at the club can be compared to the 'no dickheads' philosophy of New Zealand's national rugby union team, the All Blacks. It is based on the belief that the collective culture of a team can be spoiled by one selfish mindset.

This was demonstrated recently in Guardiola's decision to loan full-back Joao Cancelo to Bayern Munich during the winter transfer window. In January and February, journalists were speculating about the body language and mood of the players in the City dressing room.

One of those players was Cancelo, who has admitted to feeling unhappy if he didn't start every game. When Cancelo requested to leave, Guardiola was quick to oblige because he put the team above its individual members. His staff believe this was a crucial decision in improving team harmony.

Research shows that measuring the effect of a leader on organisational performance is a challenging task. This is because there are multiple factors that can cause a positive or negative impact. But without doubt, while Manchester City had won Premier League titles before the arrival of Guardiola, his leadership has transformed the team.

It has helped them to become 'hybrid monsters', who can play with any formation and any player combination and still consistently challenge for European honours.

Manchester City are yet to play in the FA Cup and UEFA Champions League finals. While they are the favourites to win both trophies, football is a funny game and nothing is certain until the final whistle is blown.

Should they emerge victorious, Manchester City will become the second English club to win the treble (League, Cup and Continental Championship) since their rivals, Manchester United, did it in 1999. They will also become the sixth English club to win the UEFA Champions League, cementing their place as one of the best football teams in history.

11.1

Activity

1 What two elements were crucial to Manchester City's sustained success?

____

2 According to research, why is measuring the effect of a leader on organisational performance a 'challenging task'? ______________________________

3 Name the coach of the team. ______________________________

4 Name three players from the team.

____

5 When Cancelo asked for permission to leave, why was Guardiola 'quick to oblige'?

____

6 What does the author mean when he describes the team as 'hybrid monsters'?

____

7 What is 'vertical integration'?

____

8 Why is vertical integration a strategic advantage?

____

9 What team did Arsenal lose to? ______________________________

10 What do you think Mondal means when he writes, 'football is a funny game and nothing is certain until the final whistle is blown'?

____

____

Comprehension focus 2: inferring, connecting, scanning and summarising

The following extract is an example of writing from the fantasy genre.

In the heart of the ancient forest, where the shadows whispered secrets only the trees could decipher ... a realm untouched by time waited patiently.

Elara moved with the grace of a phantom. Cloaked in hues of midnight that seemed to absorb the very essence of darkness, she navigated the enchanted woods with a familiarity and confidence that betrayed years of communion with the mysterious world. Her steps were as silent as the wind brushing against the leaves, each footfall a delicate dance of melding magic and nature. She had been here since the beginning.

Beneath a cascade of ebony hair that glinted with the shimmer of starlight, her eyes held a depth as profound as the universe itself. Catching the scarce light that dared to penetrate the thick canopy, those eyes, the colour of forgotten dreams, revealed a wisdom and independence that spoke of countless encounters with mystical beings. With each step she took, a soft pulse of magic emanated from her being, resonating with the very lifeblood of the mystical realm she called home.

But this was not to be the untainted sanctuary she had known for much longer …

11.2

Activity

1 Why is the first sentence of the extract so effective in engaging the reader?

____

____

2 List all the details used to characterise the protagonist.

____

____

3 How does the text suggest that the protagonist has an affinity with her home?

____

____

4 The text is written in the past **tense**. Rewrite it, changing all the verbs into present tense.

____

____

____

____

____

____

tense The form a verb takes to signal the location of a clause in time (e.g. present tense 'has' in 'Jo has a cat' locates the situation in the present; past tense 'had' in 'Jo had a cat' locates it in the past)

5 Which approach to tense do you think is more effective? Give a reason for your answer.

____

____

6 The author uses punctuation and sentence structures in interesting ways. In the extract, highlight at least one example of:

a ellipsis

b an embedded clause

c a **conjunction** to start a sentence

7 Summarise the effects of the features listed in the previous questions in the extract.

____

____

____

conjunction In a sentence, a word that joins other words, groups/phrases or clauses together in a logical relationship such as addition, time, cause or comparison. There are two types: coordinating and subordinating

Comprehension focus 3: predicting, connecting and visualising

The image below is the cover for a novel titled *No True Believers* written by Rabiah York Lumbard and published in 2020.

11.3

Activity

1 What predictions can you make about the genre or **theme** of the novel based on its cover? Provide reasons for your answer.

2 Based on the visual clues provided, what predictions can you make about the setting or time period in which the story takes place? Provide reasons for your answer.

3 How do the colours and other visual elements used in the cover design contribute to the overall atmosphere that you predict will be created in the novel?

4 What connections can you make between the central figure on the cover and the various written features, including the typography (e.g. style, size and shaping of written text)? How might these elements be relevant to the story?

5 What connections can you make between the cover design and the potential interests and preferences of a specific target **audience**?

6 Imagine you are an illustrator and graphic designer tasked with creating a book cover for a novel of your choice. In the space below, design your own novel cover that visually represents the story and captures the reader's attention. Alternatively, you could use a software program for your design and use the space below to jot down some ideas. If you can't think of a novel yourself, some suggestions for titles and genres are:

- *Whispering Shadows* by Jan-Philipp Sendker (mystery/thriller)
- *Beyond the Stars* by CI Chevron (science fiction)
- *The Painted Sky* by Alice Campion (contemporary fiction).

theme The main idea, concept or message of a text
audience An intended or assumed group of readers, listeners or viewers that a writer, designer, filmmaker or speaker is addressing

Your design should incorporate the following elements:

- title and author's name: use appropriate typography that complements the genre, theme and style of the book.
- imagery: choose colours, symbols, objects or scenes from the story that are representative of its themes.

7 Explain the choices you made in planning your novel's cover and why you predict it will be appealing to readers.

Comprehension focus 4: activating prior knowledge, inferring and connecting

The following is an edited extract from Alice Pung's *Unpolished Gem*, written when she was just out of her teens and published when she was in her mid-twenties. She tells of growing up in a Chinese-Cambodian family newly arrived in Australia and describes how her family must learn to live in an unfamiliar culture.

Wah, so many things about this new country that are so taken-for-granted! It is a country where no one walks like they have to hide. From the top floor of the Rialto building my parents see that the people below amble in a different manner, and not just because of the heat. No bomb is ever going to fall on them. No one pissing in the street, except of course in a few select suburbs. No lepers. No Khmer Rouge-type soldiers dressed like black ants prodding occupants of the Central Business District into making a mass exodus to Wangaratta ...

Here there is sweetness, and the refugees staying at the Midway Migrant Hilton hoard packets of sugar, jam and honey from the breakfast table. So used to everything being finite, irrevocably gone if one does not grab it fast enough, they are bewildered when new packets appear on the breakfast table the next day ...

The first time my mother walks into a Sims supermarket, the first moment she sees people loading the trolleys with such habitual nonchalance, she exclaims a long, drawn-out, open-mouthed 'wahhhh' of wonder ... This enormous warehouse would shock the eyeballs out of the most prosperous families in Phnom Penh! So gleaming spick-and-span clean! Such beautiful food! Such pretty packages!

'Wah, you mean anybody can come into this big food warehouse?' my ma asks in awe ...

She thinks about the ones back in Vietnam. She sees her father sleeping on the floor of the monastery, her mother selling bancao at the market. Her skin-and-bones sisters beneath the tap outside with soap powder dripping from their hair. She thinks about the ones back home who are unprocessed and waiting to be processed, unlike the meat that is stacked in tins of twelve in front of her.

11.4 Activity

1 The extract above is from a memoir. Using your prior knowledge of the memoir genre, circle the features below that you expect it to include.

figurative language	expert opinions	anecdotes
first-person pronouns	statistics	dialogue

2 Reflect on whether your response to question 1 is correct and annotate the extract to show where memoir features are evident.

a Apart from the abundance of the food on the shelves, find three other facts about the supermarket that surprise Pung's mother.

___

___

___

b Why does Pung comically call her parents' first Australian home the 'Midway Migrant Hilton'?

3 Pung uses the expression 'habitual nonchalance' to describe the attitude of some supermarket customers. What does this mean and why do you think some supermarket customers display this attitude?

4 It amazes Pung's mother that 'anybody' is free to enter the supermarket. What does this reveal about the society she has come from?

5 Pung writes about people being 'processed', a **verb** that is widely used to describe how people are accepted into Australia. Why does she link it to the tins of meat in the supermarket? What connotations, or suggestions, are evoked by making this link?

6 Do you think your own experiences, or those of your family, affect the way in which you read Pung's memoir? Why or why not?

7 Think of a time you went to a new or unfamiliar place, such as starting at a new school, visiting a different country or moving to an unfamiliar city or town. Write a short descriptive passage that reflects on aspects that surprised or interested you.

verb A word class that expresses processes that include doing, feeling, thinking, saying and relating

Comprehension focus 5: scanning and inferring

The advertisements below were produced as part of a three-year campaign titled 'Come Live Our Philausophy' and released by Tourism Australia.

11.5 Activity

1 The campaign utilises wordplay through its slogan 'Come Live Our Philausophy'. What do you think is meant by this deliberate misspelling?

____

____

2 What specific words or **phrases** in each advertisement expand on the approach of the campaign title?

____

____

3 What is the effect of using these words or phrases? Consider the message they convey and the **tone** they create.

____

____

phrase A group of words often beginning with a preposition but without a subject and verb combination (e.g. 'on the river'; 'with brown eyes')
tone The mood created by the language features used by an author and the way the text makes the reader feel

4 Who do you think is the target audience of the advertisements? Give reasons fo- your answer.

____

____

5 In what ways do the images and written features of the advertisement align with the **values** or aspirations of the target audience? Make sure you specify what these values or aspirations are.

____

____

____

values Ideas and beliefs specific to individuals and groups

Comprehension focus 6: inferring, questioning and summarising

The following extract is from the novel *The Curious Incident of the Dog in the Night-Time* by Mark Haddon. Christopher Boone, who narrates the story, is a 15-year-old boy who has trouble relating to people around him, though the specific reason for this is not stated.

In this extract, a neighbour's dog has been killed, and Christopher has hit a policeman. Christopher's father, Ed, has come to collect him from the police station.

I said, 'I'm sorry,' because Father had had to come to the police station, which was a bad thing.

He said, 'It's OK.'

I said, 'I didn't kill the dog.'

And he said, 'I know.'

Then he said, 'Christopher, you have to stay out of trouble, OK?'

I said, 'I didn't know I was going to get into trouble. I like Wellington and I went to say hello to him, but I didn't know that someone had killed him.'

Father said, 'Just try and keep your nose out of other people's business.'

I thought for a little and I said, 'I am going to find out who killed Wellington.'

And Father said, 'Were you listening to what I was saying, Christopher?'

I said, 'Yes, I was listening to what you were saying, but when someone gets murdered you have to find out who did it so that they can be punished.'

And he said, 'It's a bloody dog, Christopher, a bloody dog.'

11.6

Activity

1 What evidence in this extract suggests that Christopher thinks in a different way from his father?

____

____

2 What aspects of the extract do you find confusing or want to know more about?

____

____

The novel continues:

> I replied, 'I think dogs are important, too.'
>
> He said, 'Leave it.'
>
> And I said, 'I wonder if the police will find out who killed him and punish the person.'
>
> Then Father banged the steering wheel with his fist and the car weaved a little bit across the dotted line in the middle of the road and he shouted, 'I said leave it, for God's sake.'

3 What do you notice about the speech tags used to introduce the words spoken by each character? How do they create character and conflict in the extract?

____

____

Keep reading …

> I could tell that he was angry because he was shouting, and I didn't want to make him angry so I didn't say anything else until we got home.
>
> When we came in through the front door I went into the kitchen and got a carrot for Toby and I went upstairs and I shut the door of my room and I let Toby out and gave him the carrot. Then I turned my computer on and played 76 games of Minesweeper and did the Expert Version in 102 seconds, which was only 3 seconds off my best time which was 99 seconds.
>
> At 2.07 a.m. I decided that I wanted a drink of orange squash before I brushed my teeth and got into bed so I went downstairs to the kitchen. Father

was sitting on the sofa watching snooker on the television and drinking whisky. There were tears coming out of his eyes.

I asked, 'Are you sad about Wellington?'

He looked at me for a long time and sucked air in through his nose. Then he said, 'Yes, Christopher, you could say that. You could very well say that.'

I decided to leave him alone because when I am sad I want to be left alone. So I didn't say anything else. I just went into the kitchen and made my orange squash and took it back upstairs to my room.

4 What are three things that you are curious about in relation to the characters and plot of the novel so far? Write them here as three questions that you would like answered.

____

____

____

5 The novel is written in first-person narrative **point of view** (in which Christopher tells his own story). What evidence is there that he is likely to be an unreliable narrator?

____

____

____

6 'There were tears coming out of his eyes.' Christopher sees the physical fact of tears and tries to associate it with an emotion. Why do you think his father may be crying?

____

____

point of view The position from which the text is designed to be perceived (e.g. a narrator might take a role of first or third person, omniscient or restricted in knowledge of events or the opinion presented in a text)

7 Christopher's response to his father here – going into another room without speaking – may seem cold and uncaring. What does his reason for leaving his father alone show about him?

___

___

8 In full sentences and using your own words, summarise the events that have occurred in the novel from the three extracts that you have read.

___

___

___

___

Comprehension focus 7: activating prior knowledge, scanning and summarising

The following text is a review of a restaurant called Gourmet Haven.

The moment you step into Gourmet Haven, you're enveloped in an atmosphere of warmth and sophistication. Its contemporary decor features a blend of sleek furniture, soft lighting and tasteful artwork, creating an inviting and elegant space. The dining area is well-arranged, providing ample space between tables for privacy and comfort, and an ambience that strikes a perfect balance between relaxed and upscale.

Moreover, the service at Gourmet Haven is exemplary! From the moment you're greeted at the entrance, the staff members display professionalism, attentiveness and genuine warmth. They go above and beyond to ensure your dining experience is exceptional, catering to individual preferences and dietary restrictions. The floor staff are knowledgeable about the menu and provide insightful recommendations.

The culinary experience at Gourmet Haven is nothing short of extraordinary. Its menu offers a fusion of flavours from around the world, expertly crafted to create innovative and delectable dishes. Each plate is a work of art, meticulously presented with attention to detail. The quality of ingredients is evident in every bite, with fresh produce, premium cuts of meat, and thoughtfully sourced seafood. Flavours are well-balanced, showcasing a harmonious blend of spices, herbs, and sauces. Vegetarian, vegan and gluten-free options are also available, ensuring the menu also caters to everyone.

Gourmet Haven's menu boasts an array of standout dishes that are a testament to the chef's creativity and expertise. The 'Saffron-infused Seafood Risotto' is a symphony of flavours, combining plump prawns, tender scallops, and mussels with perfectly cooked Arborio rice, infused with the delicate aroma of saffron. The 'Miso-Glazed Black Cod' is another star dish, with its melt-in-your-mouth texture and a delicate balance of sweet and savoury flavours. For dessert, the 'Chocolate Decadence Cake' is a showstopper, rich and indulgent, paired with a tangy raspberry coulis.

Finally, this restaurant provides an exceptional dining experience that justifies its price point. While it may be categorised as an upscale restaurant, the quality of food, service, and ambience truly reflects the value for money. Portion sizes are generous, ensuring guests leave satisfied. Additionally, the attention to detail and the overall experience make it worth the price tag.

Dining at Gourmet Haven is an exquisite experience from start to finish. The combination of elegant ambience, impeccable service and exceptional cuisine truly sets it apart from other establishments.

11.7

Activity

1 The text is a restaurant review that offers an evaluation (or judgement) of a dining experience. What other types of experiences can be reviewed?

____

____

2 How are the ideas in the review effectively organised to provide a comprehensive overview of the restaurant?

____

____

3 Why do you think the reviewer has included specific examples, such as the 'Saffron-infused Seafood Risotto' and the 'Miso-Glazed Black Cod', to support their claims about the exceptional food quality?

____

____

4 Do you think the review would benefit from the integration of images? If so, what should be the content of these images, and where would they be most effectively positioned in the review?

____

____

Comprehension focus 8: inferring, questioning and visualising

The image below is a page from the graphic novel *Persepolis* created by Marjane Satrapi.

11.8 Activity

1 Annotate each separate panel of the page in the margins, noting your observations about the characters, the setting and the plot.

2 What can you infer to be the relationship between the young female character and the older couple?

____

____

3 Why do you think the male character is carrying the older female character in the final panel of the page?

____

____

4 Summarise the implied narrative of the three panels. What story do they tell?

____

____

5 Visualise the scene that you think might logically follow this one. Describe what it would look like.

____

____

Improving your writing

This unit targets the knowledge and skills that will help you to improve the quality of your writing. A particular focus is how to effectively **edit** and proofread your written responses. Practising these skills will enable you to communicate clearly with readers and to demonstrate your understanding of texts and issues.

edit To prepare, alter, adapt or refine with attention to grammar, spelling, punctuation and vocabulary

Curriculum content

Australian Curriculum content description	Content code
Use an expanded technical and academic vocabulary for precision when writing academic texts.	**AC9E10LA08**
Plan, create, edit and publish written and multimodal texts, organising, expanding and developing ideas through experimenting with text structures, language features, literary devices and multimodal features for specific purposes and audiences in ways that may be imaginative, reflective, informative, persuasive, analytical and/or critical.	**AC9E10LY06**
Use knowledge of the spelling system to spell words and to manipulate standard spelling for particular effects.	**AC9E10LY08**

Editing and proofreading

Editing and proofreading your written work are fundamental skills that need time and practise. While the terms 'editing' and 'proofreading' are sometimes used interchangeably and there is a degree of overlap between them, they are actually two distinct skills, as demonstrated in the diagram below.

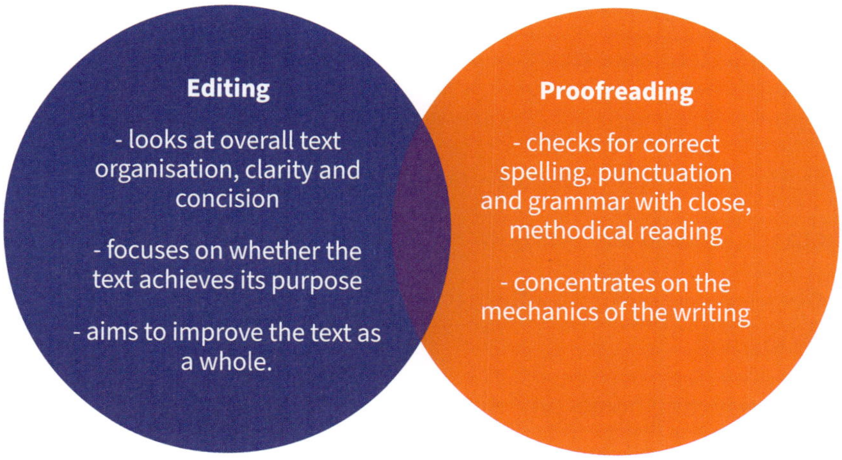

Editing

- looks at overall text organisation, clarity and concision

- focuses on whether the text achieves its purpose

- aims to improve the text as a whole.

Proofreading

- checks for correct spelling, punctuation and grammar with close, methodical reading

- concentrates on the mechanics of the writing

Whenever you do a piece of writing, keep in mind the following points.

» Whenever possible, leave time between writing a draft and the editing or proofreading processes, so that you can come back to the piece with fresh eyes.

» Read your work aloud to listen for errors and to notice areas that need improvement.

» Ensure that you edit and proofread multiple times, not just once.

» Choose a different aspect to focus on each time you edit or proofread, rather than trying to do everything at once.

» Even if you produce a piece of writing under timed conditions, allow at least a few minutes at the end of this period to quickly edit and proofread your response.

12.1

Activity

How many of the tips above do you usually apply to your own writing? Provide examples of the writing tasks that you have used them with.

Structural editing

The first aspect of your written work to concentrate on in the editing process is its overall structure and the organisation of its content.

12.2

Activity

1 What structural sequence do imaginative or creative texts generally follow?

a resolution – rising action – climax – orientation/exposition ☐

b orientation/exposition – climax – resolution – rising action ☐

c orientation/exposition – rising action – climax – resolution ☐

2 What structural sequence do informative, persuasive or analytical texts generally follow?

a hook – supporting points and evidence – call to action ☐

b supporting points and evidence – hook – call to action ☐

c call to action – supporting points and evidence – hook ☐

3 There are many ways to structure the content of a persuasive text, and these can vary according to the form of text being written. How would you choose to structure or sequence the content in a persuasive essay? Explain what you would place first, in the middle and last.

____

____

4 Apply the following editing checklist to some of your own pieces of creative and imaginative writing. Write your title and then place ticks in the right-hand columns as you carefully check each piece of writing for the elements outlined in the table.

Imaginative or creative writing editing checklist				
	Focus of edits	Title of your writing:	Title of your writing:	Title of your writing:
Plot development	› The opening exposition/orientation makes the reader want to read on. › The story builds towards an exciting climax. › The resolution ties everything together.			
Crafting of character and dialogue	› The characters are interesting and authentic. › The goals of the protagonist are clear and achievable. › The relationships between characters are well developed. › The dialogue between characters sounds believable and is balanced with narration.			
Crafting of setting	› The setting is created in a way that allows readers to picture locations. › The passing of time is conveyed clearly.			
Writing style	› The style of writing suits the text's form and genre. › Sensory details and figurative language are included to good effect.			
Narrative point of view	› The narrative point of view suits the story being told.			

5 Apply the following editing checklist to some of your own pieces of informative, persuasive or analytical writing. Write your topic and then place ticks in the right-hand columns as you carefully check each piece of writing for the elements outlined in the table.

Informative, persuasive or analytical writing editing checklist		Topic of your writing:	Topic of your writing:	Topic of your writing:
	Focus of edits			
Content	› The text responds fully to the topic or issue. › An appropriate number of ideas are developed in detail. › Ideas are supported by relevant reasons and/or evidence.			
Structure	› The introduction outlines the approach to the topic or issue. › Each idea is expanded in a separate body paragraph. › The information in each body paragraph is presented in a logical order (e.g. TEEL). › The concluding paragraph summarises the main points.			
Writing style	› The terminology and **metalanguage** used match the form and purpose of the writing. › An understanding of key words is evident in the response.			

metalanguage Vocabulary including technical terms, concepts, ideas or codes used to describe or discuss a language. The language of grammar and the language of literary criticism are examples

Improving the structure of your writing

Editing effectively will usually mean that you detect some problems with the structure and content of your written responses. Consider the problems you found when you used the checklists in the previous activity. Try the following measures to solve them.

» Remove content that does not serve the purpose of your text.

» Remove unnecessary repetition of points.

» Decide whether particular points or elements are best placed elsewhere in your response. Perhaps the evidence in one paragraph is better suited to the point in another paragraph, or maybe plot points need to be placed earlier in a story to clarify events for readers.

» Rework paragraphs or scenes if they don't make sense. Be prepared to rewrite them from scratch if they are too illogically ordered.

» Add more detail and explanation for points or plot developments that require strengthening.

12.3

Activity

1 Compare the following two openings of persuasive pieces of writing, both focused on the issue of climate change inaction.

Opening A: In today's world, there are many important issues that we need to address. Climate change is one of them. It's a big problem. Governments are ignoring the fact that the Earth is getting warmer and that's threatening us all. Carbon emissions are also increasing all the time and governments fail to act on this important issue. We need to do something about it. It's causing all sorts of problems like rising sea levels, extreme weather events and the extinction of species. We should all be concerned and take action. I mean, why wouldn't we? It's our planet, after all. We need to reduce our carbon footprint, switch to renewable energy sources and support policies that protect the environment. The government should do more, too. They need to pass laws and regulations to combat climate change. We can't just sit back and ignore this issue. The government should take responsibility now as it's urgent and requires immediate attention. Let's work together to save our planet!

Opening B: Climate change, a threat looming over our planet, demands our unwavering attention and concerted action. The consequences of our inaction are becoming increasingly evident, from the rising sea levels that imperil coastal communities to the surge in extreme weather events that ravage entire regions. The clock is ticking, and we must act swiftly and decisively to mitigate the devastating effects and secure a sustainable future.

With each passing day, our carbon emissions continue to escalate, exacerbating the greenhouse effect and driving global temperatures to alarming heights. To combat this pressing issue, a collective effort is imperative. Individually, we can reduce our carbon footprint by adopting energy-efficient practices, embracing renewable energy sources and advocating for responsible consumption patterns. However, the responsibility does not rest solely on our shoulders.

2 Which of the extracts do you think organises its content better? Provide reasons for your answer.

3 Opening B finishes with the line, 'However, the responsibility does not rest solely on our shoulders'. What idea or point do you think this naturally leads to in the paragraph that will follow?

4 Both of the sample openings could be improved with greater attention to editing for content and structure. Jot down some points about how you would improve each of them.

Opening A	Opening B

Sentence-level editing

Editing at the sentence level should take place once you have finished the task of editing the text's structure and organisation of content. Sentence-level editing is also called 'copyediting'. It helps ensure that the **style** of your writing is effective in achieving its purpose.

The following tasks form part of the sentence-level editing process.

» Ensure that your word choices match the form and purpose of your writing. For instance, slang words and contractions may need to be removed to maintain a formal register in an academic piece of writing such as an analytical essay.

» Check the clarity of each sentence, making sure that each sentence makes sense. Remove unnecessary or repetitive words and **phrases**.

style The distinctive language features, text structures and/or subject matter in a text which may shape meaning, be enjoyed for its aesthetic qualities or distinguish the work of an author, period etc.

phrase A group of words often beginning with a preposition but without a subject and verb combination (e.g. 'on the river'; 'with brown eyes')

» Make certain that you have included a variety of sentence lengths and syntactical arrangements to keep your reader interested. Shorten overly long sentences. Your writing should contain a mixture of simple, compound and **complex sentences**.

Much of the sentence-level editing process is related to achieving an appropriate writing style. The style you write in will depend on the form or text type you are creating, as well as its purpose. Sometimes the style of writing may not work well because it is too wordy or unclear.

complex sentence A sentence with one or more subordinate clauses. In the following example, the subordinate clause is shown in brackets: I took my umbrella [because it was raining]

12.4 Activity

1 Decide whether the following **adjectives** can be considered positive or negative descriptions of a writing style and provide definitions for each. You may need to use a dictionary.

Adjective to describe writing style	Positive or negative?	Definition
tautological		
verbose		
eloquent		
repetitious		
academic		
descriptive		
expressive		
evocative		
pompous		
longwinded		
convoluted		

2 What kinds of texts would you expect to be written in an academic style?

____

____

3 What kinds of texts would you expect to be written in a descriptive style?

____

____

4 Read the following extract from an imaginative short story.

> The king, a paragon of wisdom and sagacity, governed with an iron fist, yet possessed a heart brimming with compassion. His subjects, awestruck by his magnanimous presence, held him in high regard, valuing his guidance and directives above all else. In this realm, there thrived a quaint village, nestled amidst lush greenery and rolling hills, where the villagers, a close-knit community bound by unyielding ties, led a modest and tranquil existence. An idyllic haven untouched by the ravages of time, the village basked in an eternal state of serenity.

5 This extract could be improved with more variety in word choice, sentence length and syntactical arrangement. Rewrite the paragraph for an **audience** of readers your age, substituting any words that you need a dictionary to understand with more accessible terminology. Ensure that your paragraph includes both simple and **compound sentences**.

____

____

____

____

____

adjective A word class that describes, identifies or quantifies a noun or a pronoun, e.g. two (number or quantity), my (possessive), ancient (descriptive), shorter (comparative), wooden (classifying)
audience An intended or assumed group of readers, listeners or viewers that a writer, designer, filmmaker or speaker is addressing
compound sentence A sentence with 2 or more main clauses of equal grammatical status, usually marked by a coordinating conjunction, e.g. [Ira came home this morning] [but he didn't stay long]

Read the following short analytical essay paragraph.

Animal Farm just isn't for kids 'cause they just won't get all the Russian Revolution references and all that historical stuff. It could've been a bit better for them if it wasn't for what happened to poor old Boxer, but most kids would be dead-set traumatised reading of what happened to him. It's actually pretty depressing to think that's actually the kinda treatment that happened to some of the people at the time, even though they worked their backsides off.

6 Circle the adjectives below that best describe the style of writing used in the analytical paragraph above.

formal	academic	colloquial	informal
descriptive	convincing	eloquent	succinct

7 How well does the register of the paragraph match its purpose and form? Provide reasons for your answer.

____

____

8 Aim to improve the analytical paragraph by rewriting it in the space below, paying attention to the register and sentence structure in order to establish a style suited to the purpose of an analytical paragraph.

____

____

____

____

____

Proofreading for spelling

Poor spelling can compromise the meaning and the credibility of your writing, so it is important to use strategies to address this area and to learn how to spell new words. The 'look, say, cover, write, check' method can help you learn to spell unfamiliar words. Flashcards, posters and word walls can also hassist in memorising technical terms and difficult words.

When proofreading your writing for spelling mistakes, implement the following strategies:

» Check for homophone confusion, as it can be easy to confuse words that sound alike, such as 'there', 'they're' and 'their'; 'practice' and 'practise'; and 'affect' and 'effect'.

» Check for correct use of suffixes. Some of the most frequently misspelled words are those that end in suffixes such as '–ation', '–ly' and '–ed'.

» Check for words with silent (unpronounced) letters, such as 'playwright', 'mortgage' and 'psychology'.

» Check for accidental phonetic spelling, which mimics the sound of speech. For example, phonetic spelling would have you incorrectly writing 'definately' instead of 'definitely'.

» Check that you have used Australian spellings, particularly when using word-processing tools, which frequently autocorrect words to American rather than Australian spelling, such as 'favorite' instead of 'favourite' and 'color' instead of 'colour'.

» Beware of the exceptions to spelling rules. For instance, we are often taught the spelling rule 'i before e except after c', but this doesn't apply to words such as 'leisure', 'neither', 'neighbour', 'foreign, 'ancient' and many other exceptions.

12.5

Activity

1 Highlight the ten spelling /punctuation errors in the following paragraph.

Your not going to believe this but I just saw the most amazing sunset eva. The colors were so beuatiful, they took my breathe away. It is sure to become a favorite moment that I'll never forget! Its the kind of thing you read about in storys or see on television shows but never get too expereince in real life.

2 Rewrite the paragraph above using correct spelling.

____

____

____

____

3 Each pair of words below contains a frequently misspelled word and its correct spelling. Circle the correctly spelled words.

achievement / acheivement

tomorrow / tommorow

separate / seperate

definitely / definately

rythm / rhythm

arguement / argument

independent / independant

embarrass / embarass

writting / writing

4 Conduct some online research to help you complete the table below with some common spelling rules and their exceptions. One example has been done for you.

Spelling rule	Examples	Some exceptions to the rule
'i before e except after c'	believe, receive, ceiling	weird, seize, science, height

5 Sometimes, words may be deliberately misspelled in order to achieve a particular effect. Tick which of the following effects might be achieved by the manipulation of standard spelling:

a to indicate the accent of a character ☐

b to reveal that the author can't spell very well ☐

c to suggest that a character or the narrator is naive, childlike or uneducated ☐

d to mimic a particular sound or noise ☐

e for comical effect ☐

f to create a pun or engaging wordplay ☐

6 Select any three effects from those you ticked above and for each one either find or create your own sentence that includes deliberately misspelled words to achieve the effect chosen.

a ____

____

b ____

____

c ____

____

Proofreading for grammar

Checking your written work closely to correct any grammatical errors is also an important part of the proofreading process. Look for the following elements during this phase.

Check that all sentences are complete, in that they contain a **subject** and a **verb**. Correct any sentence fragments, which are incomplete sentences. For example:

» running for the bus. (fragment; incorrect)

» I was running late for the bus. (complete sentence; correct)

Check for accidental run-on sentences, in which two or more sentences are incorrectly combined, often with a comma in the middle. For example:

» The writer includes an expert opinion, this adds credibility to their argument. (run-on sentence; incorrect)

» The writer includes an expert opinion. This technique adds credibility to their argument. (correct)

or

» The writer includes an expert opinion, adding credibility to their argument. (correct)

subject A word or group of words (usually a noun group/phrase) in a sentence or clause representing the person, thing or idea doing the action that follows (e.g. 'The dog [subject] was barking')
verb A word class that expresses processes that include doing, feeling, thinking, saying and relating

12.6

Activity

1 Label the following sentences as either complete, fragments or run-on sentences:

a I went to the supermarket to buy groceries, I also needed to pick up some cleaning supplies, my neighbours joined me on the drive. ______________

b While I was walking in the park. ______________

c She baked a delicious cake for her friend's birthday. ______________

d Because it was raining heavily. ______________

e At the knock on the door, the dog barked loudly. ______________

f The concert was amazing, the band played all of their hit songs. ______________

2 Check one of your own pieces of writing, ensuring that all sentences are complete and correctly punctuated. Rewrite fragments or run-on sentences as complete sentences.

Check subject-verb agreement so that the subject/s in a sentence correspond to the verb/s in number. For example:

» The friends was enjoying their holiday. (incorrect verb)

» The friends were enjoying their holiday. (correct verb)

Check **tenses**. It is common to incorrectly shift from one tense to another. For example:

tense The form a verb takes to signal the location of a clause in time (e.g. present tense 'has' in 'Jo has a cat' locates the situation in the present; past tense 'had' in 'Jo had a cat' locates it in the past)

» She enters the room hesitantly. Looking around her, she noticed the strange mist. (incorrect; shifts from present to past tense)

» She enters the room hesitantly. Looking around her, she notices the strange mist. (correct; maintains present tense)

12.7

Activity

1 Read the following passage and edit it for accidental run-on sentences, fragments, subject-verb disagreement and incorrect tenses.

> The concert were amazing last night, the band played all of their hit songs. Singing along and dancing. The lead singer's voice were incredible and the guitar solos was mind-blowing. Me and my friends, we had the best time ever, it was a night we will never forget. The atmosphere is electric and the crowd were going wild. They performed for over two hours non-stop, their energy was contagious.

2 Select a piece of your own narrative writing and edit it carefully to ensure that the verbs agree with their subjects and that the tense is maintained throughout.

3 Provide an example of a sentence you have written that demonstrates your understanding of subject-verb agreement.

____

____

4 What tense have you chosen to use in your chosen narrative? ________________

5 Record five of the verbs you have used in your narrative that maintain this tense.

____

Although checking for and rectifying grammatical errors such as those outlined above will improve your writing, it is important to remember that sometimes unconventional and 'incorrect' sentences can be deliberately used by writers to achieve particular effects.

For example, sentence fragments can be used in creative, imaginative pieces or persuasive texts to control the pace of the writing, to emphasise a point or to create a particular atmosphere.

Activity

1 Find an example of a sentence fragment in a fictional narrative or within a persuasive speech. Write the fragment in the space below.

____

2 Explain the effect of the sentence fragment. Consider the **context** of the other sentences that surround it and the purpose it serves.

____

____

context An environment or situation (social, cultural or historical) in which a text is responded to or created. Or wording surrounding an unfamiliar word, which a reader or listener uses to understand its meaning

Proofreading for punctuation and capitalisation

Punctuation can also play a significant role in creating meaning in writing. There is a big difference between 'Let's eat Grandma' and 'Let's eat, Grandma' and between 'Crocodiles! Don't swim here!' and 'Crocodiles don't swim here!' When proofreading with a focus on punctuation, look out for the following aspects.

Check that you have used capital letters for proper nouns, including the names of people, places and organisations.

Check that dialogue is punctuated correctly by enclosing it within speech, or quotation marks. Begin dialogue with a capital letter unless it is the continuation of a sentence started prior to the speech tag. For example:

» 'Take a jacket,' Mum called, 'so you don't catch a cold. It's freezing outside!'

Check that apostrophes are used only to indicate possession (e.g. Raina's bag) or to indicate missing letters in a **contraction**.

Make sure you haven't inadvertently written 'it's' as 'its' or vice versa. The word 'its' is a short possessive **pronoun**, just like 'his' or 'her' (e.g. the cat couldn't believe its luck when the mouse ran straight in front of it). With an apostrophe, 'it's' is a contraction, short for 'it is' (e.g. it's going to be a chilly day).

contraction An abbreviated version of a word or words, often formed by shortening a word or merging 2 words into one (e.g. doctor: Dr; do not: don't)

pronoun A word that takes the place of a noun (e.g. I, me, he, she, herself, you, it, that, they, few, many, who, whoever, someone, everybody, and many others)

Check your use of commas. The most common uses of commas are:

- to separate items in a list (e.g. She collected eggs, apples, bread and milk from the shop.)
- to separate a subordinate **clause** or phrase from a main clause (e.g. Waiting impatiently for the shop to open, I paced around like a caged bear.)
- to indicate when you are directly addressing someone (e.g. Candice, it was so great to see you yesterday.)
- to separate dialogue from a speech tag (e.g. Mum replied, 'I'll get there as soon as I can.').

As with grammar, sentence structure and spelling, sometimes writers deliberately manipulate punctuation **conventions** and subvert rules in order to create effects. While you might try to do the same, it is very important that these manipulations are purposeful rather than accidental or simply used as an excuse to mask poor writing.

clause A grammatical unit referring to a happening or state e.g. 'the team won' (happening), 'the dog is red' (state), usually containing a subject and a verb group/phrase
convention An accepted practice that has developed over time and is generally used and understood (e.g. use of punctuation)

12.9 Activity

1 Highlight the punctuation errors in the paragraph below.

The novel was written by acclaimed author, stephanie singh it tells the story of a young protagonist named nash who embarks on a perilous journey to discover the truth about his mysterious past! The Main Character encounter's a series of challenges triumphs and adventures; finally meeting their fate at the end the narrative is filled with suspense and intrigue creating a sense of anticipation excitement and imagination in the reader's mind. it explores complex themes such as identity redemption and the blurred line's between good and evil. Its a thought-provoking and emotionally resonant piece of literature.

2 Draw lines in the table below to match the names of the punctuation marks in the left-hand column with their matching symbols in the middle column.

Name of punctuation mark	Symbol	Example
ellipsis	:	
semicolon	( )	
colon	…	
dash	-	
hyphen	–	
parentheses	;	

3 In the right-hand column of the table above, write an example sentence that correctly includes the type of punctuation mark named in the left-hand column.

semicolon Punctuation (;) used to join closely related clauses that could stand alone as sentences and can be used to separate long items in a list
colon Punctuation mark (:) that separates a general statement from one or more statements that give extra information, explanation or illustration. Statements after a colon do not have to be full sentences

Research

Including evidence of research can help improve the quality of your writing, particularly in informative, persuasive and analytical responses. Research can be divided into two broad categories: primary research and secondary research.

Primary research is carried out by accessing unedited, firsthand written or oral testimonies, images or objects created by a person or group directly involved in the event or present at the time that is being researched. Sources of primary research include emails, interviews, photographs, speeches and government files or databases.

Secondary research is carried out by accessing commentaries, analyses or interpretations of events, topics or people. A disadvantage of secondary research sources is that they are not usually created by people directly involved in an event or present at a particular time. Some advantages are that they are created by experts in a field and can provide a broader historical **perspective**.

perspective A lens through which the author perceives the world and creates a text, or the lens through which the reader or viewer perceives the world and understands a text

Research tips

Understand your task. If you have been given a topic or question to research, identify all of its key terms. Then create a list of questions or main points to focus on in your final piece.

Make a list of possible sources of information. These might include the internet, a school or public library, organisations, newspapers, journals or public records.

Think critically. Make notes from your sources, carefully considering the validity of all information or ideas you find. Ask yourself:

- What is the source of this information?
- Is it likely to be reliable and unbiased?
- What supporting evidence exists for this information or point of view?

As you do your research, ensure that you record the bibliographical details of your information sources to use later in your referencing.

Analyse and organise your information. This means:

- identifying relevant information
- recognising patterns in the information you have gathered so that you can group similar items together (you may find it helpful to write a list of relevant subheadings for your topic on separate pages or in a grid to sort information throughout the research process)
- arranging your ideas and information logically to support your argument and/or to respond to your topic.

12.10

Activity

1 Brainstorm a list of English tasks or assessments you have completed for which you needed to conduct research.

2 Why do you think providing evidence of research in your written responses improves them?

Adding multimodal elements

Sometimes, your work can be improved with the addition of different modes of communication; this may even be a requirement of some tasks.

Other communication modes include:

- visual elements like props, pictures, photographs, graphs, maps etc.
- spoken language
- audio material
- body language and gesture
- spatial elements, such as the arrangement of objects on a page or screen.

12.11

Activity

1 What do you think is the advantage of using multimodal elements when this is appropriate to a task?

____

____

Multimodal texts allow you to be very creative how you present information. You can deliver it as a live reading or presentation, printed on paper or in electronic form. Some of the most common multimodal texts are outlined below, but you do not necessarily need to limit yourself to these when asked to create a multimodal text.

Poster: a familiar multimodal form using both written and visual **language features**. The layout is particularly important when creating a poster, as you need to present an eye-catching balance of text and illustration.

Webpage: combines visual and written elements, allowing readers to interact with the text and explore it in their own way. In creating a webpage, remember that the information you present is the most important aspect.

Slide show: a popular choice for presenting information or demonstrating understanding of a topic through multimodal features. Slide shows can supplement oral presentations or work successfully as stand-alone texts.

multimodal A combination of 2 or more communication modes (e.g. print, image and spoken text, as in film or computer presentations)
language features Features that support meaning e.g. clause- and word-level grammar, vocabulary, figurative language, punctuation, images. Choices vary for the purpose, subject matter, audience and mode or medium

2 When creating multimodal texts, it is important to consider the aspects listed below so that the texts do not become cluttered and difficult to follow. Complete the table with a focus on elements used in multimodal texts. The table has been started for you.

Element	Definition	Relevant text forms	Important considerations
layout	the way in which different components are designed, arranged; composition	› posters › webpages › slide shows	achieving balance; minimal text so it is easy to read and eye-catching
transitions			
salience			
typography			
colour			
hyperlinks			
headings			

Technical and academic terminology

Your writing can be improved considerably by the deliberate choice of technical and academic terminology. An expanded vocabulary will help you achieve precision when writing academic texts such as reports, reviews and analytical essays. In English, the language we use to analyse language is called ‘metalanguage’.

The following list gives examples of general vocabulary and possible alternative terms that are more technical or academic.

General vocabulary		Technical or academic vocabulary
the start of the story	→	the establishment of the narrative
the most eye-catching part of the ad	→	the salient feature of the advertisement
the end of the report	→	the report's conclusion
the story's main character and bad guy	→	the novel's protagonist and antagonist
making sounds and pictures	→	creation of auditory and visual imagery

12.12 Activity

1 Place the following metalanguage terms in full sentences that demonstrate your understanding of them. Conduct some research if necessary.

a analogy: ______________________________

____

b archetype: ______________________________

____

c connotation: ______________________________

____

d contention: ______________________________

____

e denotation: ______________________________

____

f foreshadowing: ______________________________

____

g pragmatics: ______________________________

____

h juxtaposition: ______________________________

____

i metonymy: ______________________________

____

j Brainstorm your own list of additional English metalanguage terms.

____

____

____

The technical and academic terminology we use in our writing can depend on our **purpose** for writing and the type of text being created or analysed.

2 Complete the following table by adding examples of precise vocabulary that you might be expected to use in an academic analysis of each type of text. Some words have been added to get you started.

Magazine cover	Newspaper article
cover lines	byline
Novel or short story	**Feature article**
narrative point of view	anecdote
Feature film	**Documentary film**
camera angle	archival footage
Persuasive speech	**Drama script**
call to action	stage directions

purpose An intended or assumed reason for a type of text

Glossary

adjective A word class that describes, identifies or quantifies a noun or a pronoun, e.g. two (number or quantity), my (possessive), ancient (descriptive), shorter (comparative), wooden (classifying).

adverb A word class that may modify a verb (e.g. 'softly' in 'the boy sings softly'), an adjective (e.g. 'really' in 'he is really strong') or another adverb (e.g. 'very' in 'the toddler walks very slowly').

aesthetic Concerned with a sense of beauty or an appreciation of artistic expression.

alliteration A recurrence of the same consonant sounds at the beginning of words in close succession (e.g. 'ripe, red raspberry').

assonance The repetition of vowel sounds within words (e.g. rain, main).

attitudes Particular ways of thinking and feeling towards people or things.

audience An intended or assumed group of readers, listeners or viewers that a writer, designer, filmmaker or speaker is addressing.

cinematography The science and art of shooting motion-picture scenes, including the camera work and lighting.

clause A grammatical unit referring to a happening or state e.g. 'the team won' (happening), 'the dog is red' (state), usually containing a subject and a verb group/phrase.

cohesion Grammatical or lexical relationships that bind different parts of a text together and give it unity. It is achieved through devices such as reference, substitution, repetition and text connectives.

colon Punctuation mark (:) that separates a general statement from one or more statements that give extra information, explanation or illustration. Statements after a colon do not have to be full sentences.

complex sentence A sentence with one or more subordinate clauses. In the following example, the subordinate clause is shown in brackets: I took my umbrella [because it was raining].

compound sentence A sentence with 2 or more main clauses of equal grammatical status, usually marked by a coordinating conjunction, e.g. [Ira came home this morning] [but he didn't stay long].

comprehension strategies Processes used by readers to make meaning from texts. They include activating and using prior knowledge, predicting likely future events in a text, monitoring meaning and critically reflecting.

conjunction In a sentence, a word that joins other words, groups/phrases or clauses together in a logical relationship such as addition, time, cause or comparison. There are 2 types: coordinating and subordinating.

connective Words linking, and logically relating ideas to one another, in paragraphs and sentences indicating relationships of time, cause and effect, comparison, addition, condition and concession or clarification.

context An environment or situation (social, cultural or historical) in which a text is responded to or created. Or wording surrounding an unfamiliar word, which a reader or listener uses to understand its meaning.

contraction An abbreviated version of a word or words, often formed by shortening a word or merging 2 words into one (e.g. doctor: Dr; do not: don't).

convention An accepted practice that has developed over time and is generally used and understood (e.g. use of punctuation).

dialect Form of a language distinguished by features of vocabulary, grammar and pronunciation particular to a region.

edit To prepare, alter, adapt or refine with attention to grammar, spelling, punctuation and vocabulary.

hybrid text A composite text resulting from a purposeful mixing of elements from different sources or genres (e.g. 'infotainment').

idiom An expression whose meaning does not relate to the literal meaning of its words (e.g. 'They went out to paint the town red').

imagery Visually descriptive or figurative language to represent things including objects, actions and ideas in ways that appeal to the senses of the reader or viewer.

imperative verb A verb that gives an order or instruction (e.g. 'open the door').

jargon Technical words specific to a certain group, such as medical or legal jargon.

language features Features that support meaning e.g. clause- and word-level grammar, vocabulary, figurative language, punctuation, images. Choices vary for the purpose, subject matter, audience and mode or medium.

literary text Past and contemporary texts across a range of cultural contexts which are valued for their form and style and are recognised as having artistic value.

metalanguage Vocabulary including technical terms, concepts, ideas or codes used to describe or discuss a language. The language of grammar and the language of literary criticism are examples.

metaphor A type of figurative language used to describe a person or object through an implicit comparison to something with similar characteristics.

mise en scène In film, the composition of a shot, including elements such as lighting, costumes, props, set design and special effects.

modal verb A verb that expresses a degree of probability attached by a speaker or writer to a statement (e.g. 'I might come home') or a degree of obligation (e.g. 'You must give it to me').

mode Various processes of communication – listening, speaking, reading or viewing and writing or creating.

multimodal A combination of 2 or more communication modes (e.g. print, image and spoken text, as in film or computer presentations).

narrative The selection and sequencing of events or experiences, real or imagined, to tell a story to entertain, engage, inform and extend imagination, typically using an orientation, complication and resolution.

noun A word class that includes all words denoting person, place, object or thing, idea or emotion. Nouns may be common, proper, collective, abstract and compound.

perspective A lens through which the author perceives the world and creates a text, or the lens through which the reader or viewer perceives the world and understands a text.

phrase A group of words often beginning with a preposition but without a subject and verb combination (e.g. 'on the river'; 'with brown eyes').

point of view The position from which the text is designed to be perceived (e.g. a narrator might take a role of first or third person, omniscient or restricted in knowledge of events or the opinion presented in a text)

prefix A meaningful element (morphemes) added to the beginning of a word to change its meaning (e.g. 'un' to 'happy' to make 'unhappy').

preposition A word class that usually describes the relationship between words in a sentence. Prepositions can indicate space (e.g. 'on'), time (e.g. 'after') and other relationships (e.g. 'of', 'except').

prepositional phrase A group of words that typically consists of a preposition followed by a noun group/phrase (e.g. 'on the train' in 'we met on the train'; 'on golf' in 'keen on golf').

pronoun A word that takes the place of a noun (e.g. I, me, he, she, herself, you, it, that, they, few, many, who, whoever, someone, everybody, and many others).

protagonist The main character in a text.

purpose An intended or assumed reason for a type of text.

salience A strategy of emphasis, highlighting what is important in a text. In images, it is achieved through strategies such as the placement of an item in the foreground, size and contrast in tone or colour.

scan To read, moving one's eyes quickly down a page seeking specific words and phrases. It is also used when a reader first finds information to determine whether it will answer their questions.

semicolon Punctuation (;) used to join closely related clauses that could stand alone as sentences and can be used to separate long items in a list.

simile A device comparing 2 things that are not alike. Similes use 'like', 'as' or 'than' to make the comparison (e.g. The cake was as light as air).

skim Reading quickly, selecting key words and details through a text to determine the general meaning or main messages or ideas.

Standard Australian English Recognised as the 'common language' of Australians, it is the dynamic and evolving spoken and written English used for official or public purposes, and recorded in dictionaries, style guides and grammars.

style The distinctive language features, text structures and/or subject matter in a text which may shape meaning, be enjoyed for its aesthetic qualities or distinguish the work of an author, period etc.

subject A word or group of words (usually a noun group/phrase) in a sentence or clause representing the person, thing or idea doing the action that follows (e.g. 'The dog [subject] was barking').

subject matter The topic or theme under consideration.

subordinating conjunction Words that introduce clauses that add or extend information. They include conjunctions such as 'after', 'when', 'because', 'if' and 'that'.

suffix An element added to the end of a word to change its meaning (e.g. to form past tense: '-ed'; to show a smaller amount or degree: -less; to form an adverb: -ly).

symbolism The use of one object, person or situation to signify or represent another by giving them meanings that are different from their literal sense (e.g. a dove is a symbol of peace).

synonym A word having nearly the same meaning as others (e.g. synonyms for 'old' include 'aged', 'venerable', 'antiquated').

tense The form a verb takes to signal the location of a clause in time (e.g. present tense 'has' in 'Jo has a cat' locates the situation in the present; past tense 'had' in 'Jo had a cat' locates it in the past).

theme The main idea, concept or message of a text.

tone The mood created by the language features used by an author and the way the text makes the reader feel.

values Ideas and beliefs specific to individuals and groups.

verb A word class that expresses processes that include doing, feeling, thinking, saying and relating.

verb group Consists of a main verb, alone or preceded by one or more auxiliary or modal verbs as modifiers.

visual features Visual components of a text which may include placement, salience, framing, representation of action or reaction, shot size, social distance and camera angle.

voice The distinct personality of a piece of writing; the individual writing style of the composer, created through the way they use and mix various language features (e.g. a narrative using a child's voice).

Acknowledgements

Insight Publications thanks the following writers for their contributions to *Australian Curriculum English Year 10*: Leanne Bondin and Adam Kealley. Thank you to Avril Good for her assistance with the Victorian grids.

Insight Publications is also grateful to the following individuals and organisations for permission to reproduce copyright material.

Texts: Extract: 'Laugh, Kookaburra' by David Sedaris, David Sedaris and Don Congdon Associates; Poem: 'Be Good, Little Migrants' by Uyen Loewald in *Growing up Asian in Australia*, Black Inc.; Poem: 'Warning' by Jenny Joseph, © Jenny Joseph, reproduced with permission of Johnson & Alcock Ltd.; 'An oasis of friendship grows with the vegies', The Sydney Morning Herald; Extract: 'Is this the future of food? 'Seven West Media (WA) | The West Australian; Extract: 'Rainbow's End', by Jane Harrison, Cleven V., Enoch, W., & Milroy, D. (eds), *Contemporary Indigenous plays*, Currency Press (2007); Speech extract: TEDx event in Melbourne in 2015 by Thomas King; Extract: *Illegal* by Eoin Colfer and Andrew Donkin, illustrated by Giovanni Rigano, Hachette UK; Extract: *Shadows on the Nile* by Kate Furnivall, Hatchette UK (2012); 'Manchester City: how Pep Guardiola's leadership style formed a squad of champions' by Sarthak Mondal, University of Portsmouth, *The Conversation*; Extract: *Unpolished Gem* by Alice Pung, Black Inc.; Excerpt(s) from THE CURIOUS INCIDENT OF THE DOG IN THE NIGHT-TIME: A NOVEL by Mark Haddon, copyright © 2003 by Mark Haddon. Used by permission of Doubleday, an imprint of the Knopf Doubleday Publishing Group, a division of Penguin Random House LLC. All rights reserved; Extract: Persepolis: *The Story of a Childhood* by Marjane Satrapi, Penguin Random House.

Images: Image: 'Alternative food images'; Seven West Media (WA) | The West Australian; Cover image: 'Animal Farm', Barrington Stoke – © Barrington Stoke, 2023; Infographic: 'Sustainable Fish', Do Something! Foodwise; Infographic: 'Discovering your learning style', dailyinfographic.com.; Infographic: '7-different-types-of-learning-styles', elearninginfogaphics.com.; Infographic: 'Whats-your-learning-style', elearninginfogaphics.com.; Cover and internal images : *Illegal* by Eoin Colfer and Andrew Donkin, illustrated by Giovanni Rigano, Hachette UK; Images: *The Boat* adapted by Matt Huynh, SBS; Cover Image: *No True Believers* by Rabiah York, Penguin Books UK; Advertisements: 'Come Live Our Philausophy' by Tourism Australia: